Big Daddy's Zubba Bubba Holiday BBQ

Rick Marx

Roadside Amusements
an imprint of Chamberlain Bros.
a member of Penguin Group (USA) Inc.
New York
2005

ROADSIDE AMUSEMENTS
an imprint of
CHAMBERLAIN BROS.
Published by the Penguin Group
Penguin Group (USA) Inc., 375 Hudson Street,
New York, New York 10014, USA
Penguin Group (Canada), 90 Eglinton Avenue East, Suite 700, Toronto, Ontario
M4P 2Y3, Canada (a division of Pearson Penguin Canada Inc.)
Penguin Books Ltd, 80 Strand, London WC2R 0RL, England
Penguin Ireland, 25 St Stephen's Green, Dublin 2,
Ireland (a division of Penguin Books Ltd)
Penguin Group (Australia), 250 Camberwell Road, Camberwell, Victoria 3124,
Australia (a division of Pearson Australia Group Pty Ltd)
Penguin Books India Pvt Ltd, 11 Community Centre, Panchsheel Park,
New Delhi–110 017, India
Penguin Group (NZ), Cnr Airborne and Rosedale Roads, Albany,
Auckland 1310, New Zealand (a division of Pearson New Zealand Ltd)
Penguin Books (South Africa) (Pty) Ltd, 24 Sturdee Avenue,
Rosebank, Johannesburg 2196, South Africa

Penguin Books Ltd, Registered Offices: 80 Strand, London WC2R 0RL, England

Library of Congress Cataloging-in-Publication Data

Marx, Rick.
  Big daddy's zubba bubba holiday BBQ / Rick Marx.
      p. cm.
  ISBN 1-59609-166-5 (pbk.)
  1. Barbecue cookery. 2. Holiday cookery. I. Title.
    TX840.B3M383   2005   2005051003
    641.5'68—dc22

Printed in the United States of America
10 9 8 7 6 5 4 3 2 1

Book design by Jaime Putorti • Title logotype adapted from a design by Mike Rivilis

The recipes contained in this book are to be followed exactly as written. The publisher is not
responsible for your specific health or allergy needs that may require medical supervision. The
publisher is not responsible for any adverse reactions to the recipes contained in this book.

While the author has made every effort to provide accurate telephone numbers and Internet
addresses at the time of publication, neither the publisher nor the author assumes any
responsibility for errors, or for changes that occur after publication. Further, the publisher
does not have any control over and does not assume any responsibility for author or third-
party websites or their content.

CONTENTS

INTRODUCTION

What's your favorite holiday? For me, they are all tied in to memories of food, delicious meals, and groups of friends filling up with food and drink. Lots of laughs, lots of family, lots of magic moments, and tastes that stick in the memory. Every gathering is reason enough to break away from the couch, step outside, and show everyone who's boss by living up to your birthright and firing up the grill (don't let the wife know that you know who the boss really is . . . it's best for everyone if you keep your mouth shut on this one). Some folks are just waking up to the realization that BBQ is more than a summer occasion, it's a year-round lifestyle. If you live up North, don't let that stop you. If you live someplace where the weather is always warm and balmy, God bless. Either way, the coals are going to be hot, so there's nothing to prevent you from going out there and doing what needs to be done, whether you're in New York or North Carolina, Boston or Butte, Minnesota or Mississippi. Trust me, turn one winter holiday over to your inner grill-master and you'll be decking the halls with hickory and charcoal for years to come.

Kick off the holiday season with a Thanksgiving barbecue. You'll find yourself waiting for this moment year-round. Why? Four words: turkey on the grill. There's nothing quite like it, and no better way to prepare the big bird than by doing it outside. You've got a ton of options to make your Turkey Day a memorable one, and we'll tell you about a few of them inside.

On the first day of Christmas, we made a Christmas lamb. On the second day, we cooked a goose. On the third, we ate leftovers, but on the fourth, we were back at the grill. On New Year's Eve, we cooked lobsters on the grill—let us show you how!

Memorial Day is the Big Mamajama of grilling, a time when everyone comes over, the first flush of spring has given way to the bouquet of summer, and it's finally warm enough to go outside and fire up the grill without a winter coat. This is the time that people begin to shift their mind-set from winter hibernation to summer fun, and they are ready to let go. That's why you, the man behind the grill, have to take action and kick pork butt by preparing the best fire-roasted meals possible. That means ribs, steaks, burgers, and franks—preferably all of the above, with half a dozen sides to boot.

Then there's the Fourth of July. For that holiday, many of us go for the franks and burgers. Personally, we prefer to make the franks and burgers on the third and the fifth of July. On the Fourth we put together the best grilled chicken you have ever eaten. More on that later. And you'll read about some special recipes for corn that will blow you away. Corn on the grill? Yeah, you bet. Don't let anybody tell you otherwise—we don't want to hear about you putting it in a pot of boiling water. No way. We'll tell you more about that too.

On Labor Day, you're not supposed to work, so we'll let you take it easy and we'll make some fun stuff that anyone can do. . . .

You see, there isn't a holiday we won't miss behind the grill—even St. Paddy's Day! Have you ever heard of brisket on the grill? We've got a mouthwatering recipe that will blow you away, and with a glass of Guinness on the side, you'll share a touch of the blarney!

We'll take you on a world tour of some unique cuisines and festivities. We'll even give you the opportunity to make your own festive occasion, where you can toast and dine in style.

So the next time you find yourself faced with a large, hungry gathering in search of good eating, whether they're celebrating, honoring, or just following the calendar, you'll be ready. Dig out the pit, fire up the grill, load up the smoker, or whatever it takes to bring your meat and fire closer together, and when they ask you why you're standing outside in the middle of a blizzard with a pair of tongs and the biggest cut of holiday meat they've ever seen—you tell 'em Big Daddy sent you!

Author Rick Marx, modeling the stylish Zubba Bubba apron.

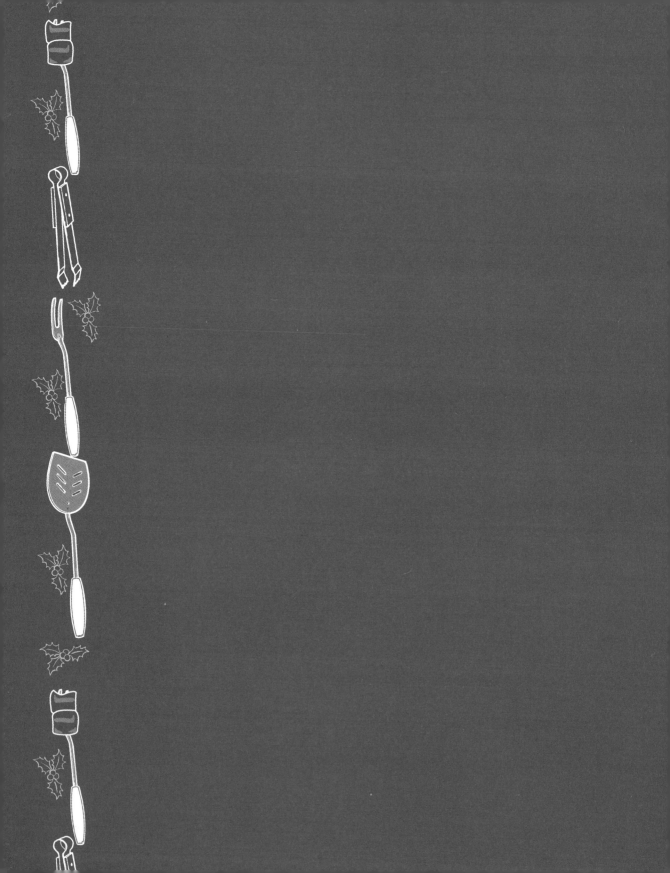

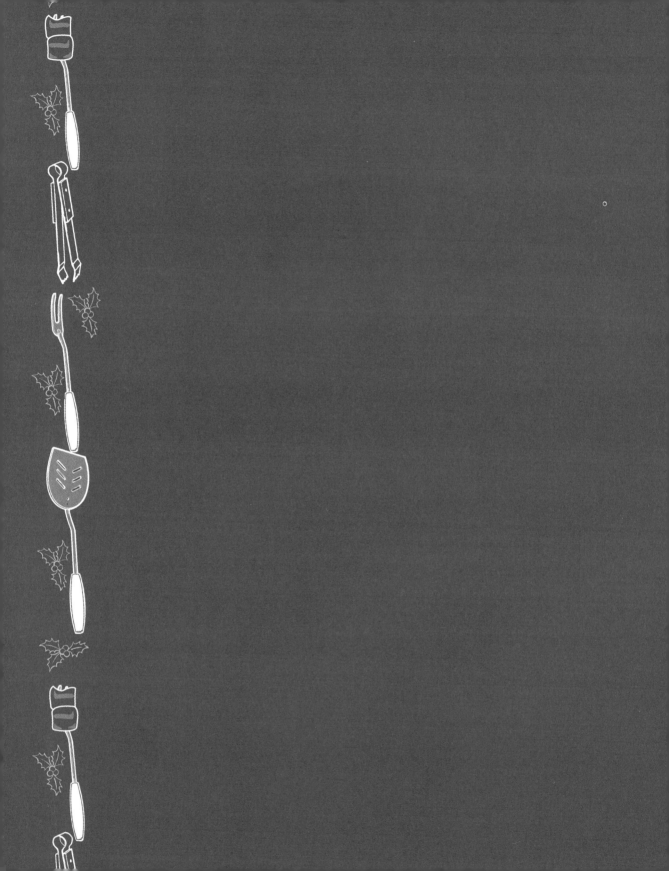

Chapter 1

Secrets of Holiday Grilling

Who wants to go to Aunt Zelda's again for the holiday? Not me. I can have my pals and friends together around the homestead year-round, and everybody's glad to pay me a visit. That's because we've got the best holiday grill parties going.

At first it was just family. Then it was family and friends. Then it was more family and friends, and before you could say "Arbor Day," we kicked some serious rump roast cooking steaks, burgers, dogs, and just about anything else that comes to mind. If you think that you can prepare the basics, now's the time to hone your skills and take it to the next step, because if you're like me, you know that outdoor grilling provides an opportunity for friends, family, fun, and a blowout party.

Along with their increased investment in equipment and supplies, a lot of folks out there—women and men—are taking cooking classes, reading cookbooks, watching the Food Network, and getting themselves in top cooking shape. You don't have to head out to the nearest grill-off or championship, but you should be wise to the great tools at your disposal. Equipment and materials allow bigger, better, and more complex grilling methods than ever before.

LET'S GET STARTED!

It used to be we had two couples over for dinner. Now we are serving a dozen. So when you prepare a meal for your pals, it's got to be more than a meal, it's got to be a feast. The prospect can be a little overwhelming—and costly, to boot. So let's keep it simple and find out what it takes to get your holiday grilling experience on the move.

Most grill books and aficionados have spent entirely too much of their time arguing about which is better, gas or charcoal. The debate is endless, and everyone has an opinion. Some people swear that food on the gas grill just doesn't have that real char-grilled flavor; gas aficionados say that gas grills are more flexible and can be fired up in no time, while a charcoal grill demands more warm-up and attention.

The truth is: they're both right. Today, especially for holiday grilling where you're preparing a variety of dishes and sides, having gas and charcoal is the key. Dave and Jim Raneri of Charles Department Store in Katonah, New York, are two of the most knowledgeable grill men I've ever met. They sell hundreds of grills, and they go to great lengths to make sure they have the latest in equipment. Yet they recommend a fairly simple setup, such as an 18¼-inch Big Green Egg charcoal grill, and a gas grill like a Weber, Broilmaster, or Ducane, which will have at least 425 square inches of cooking space.

If you are cooking for a lot of people and making a number of different courses, you may want a larger grill. So as a result, people are automatically stepping up to 505 or 650 square inches, or even larger. For a griller/smoker combo, consider a Brinkmann Smoke 'n' Grill, where large cuts of meat can be smoked rather than grilled, making them tender, juicy, and tasty. It's versatile enough to grill the old-fashioned way, too. Judge your needs, and remember you can always get more or bigger equipment. Prices can range from under $100 and skyrocket into the thousands. Get what you need but don't overbuy. It's like getting an SUV that seats nine for only three kids.

LIGHTING UP

For starting fires in a kettle, use a chimney starter, newspaper, and natural charcoal. You can use peat squares or paraffin, which you light and put under the charcoal. Be careful of electric starters, because the charcoal is often hotter than the electric starter, and once it gets past that point it's going to melt the starter. For fuel, stick with natural ingredients, such as lump charcoal, as opposed to briquettes, which have bonders and are usually chemically driven. The heat curve on a briquette is more even, but they are filled with chemicals. And lighter fluid and coated briquettes, which destroy the ozone layer, are prohibited by law in many places.

BRING ON THE HOLIDAYS!

Come the holidays, when better to spend time at home? And being outside? Winters are long. Some folks make them longer by scoffing that they won't barbecue after October. You don't have to fumble for an excuse—next winter, get out and barbecue. Keep a shovel out there, make a path, and get cooking!

Once you've made the decision to invite your friends for the big cookout, you can take advantage of all the foods at your disposal. Don't limit yourself to meat or poultry, since night after night of burgers is going to get old fast. Not only are people preparing traditional fare like ribs, chicken, and beef on the grill, but they're making vegetables, fish, many different kinds of sides, even pizzas, breads, and desserts.

Use your butcher or supermarket to best advantage. Order your meat, poultry, or fish in advance and have it prepared the way you like it for easiest cooking and serving. You can order a boned turkey breast, or a duck, Cornish hen, leg of lamb, pork shoulder, or pork butt, cut and trimmed to your liking. Choose your fish carefully, and know which ones taste best on the grill. We prefer salmon, monkfish, swordfish, and tuna. (Buy sushi-grade tuna and cook it rare—otherwise you're just a tablespoon of mayo away from tuna salad.)

Prepare your food in the kitchen in advance, especially if you are preparing a feast. Consider which type of fire to use to get the maximum experience. Place grilled vegetables on the gas grill, along with quick dishes like chicken or lamb shish kebabs. You can simultaneously do a good-sized pork loin on the kettle, or four or five racks of ribs. It's something that you can cook slowly for a few hours and you don't have to stand over it. It still has that charcoal flavor to it, and it won't get burnt.

You might cook a leg of lamb on the charcoal grill indirectly and season it up to your liking, but then in between the time it's cooking (anywhere between 90 minutes and two hours) you could make wood-fired pizzas over the charcoal fire. Simultaneously you could add vegetables on the gas grill to put onto the pizza. All these little meals build up into many different courses, alongside or instead of your main dish.

On the gas grill, do slow cooking, like a leg of lamb or a turkey breast on a rack. Remember, when you're cooking with gas, just because you've got the dial set to medium doesn't mean that the temperature is going to be on medium all the time—temperatures will fluctuate up and down, which can cause the food to dry out, which is why it's important to keep a meat thermometer handy. Also, be aware of your grill's "hot spots"—every grill has them—and cook accordingly.

One other method to cook with fire is to use a plank, which produces a whole different flavor. It's perfect for fish, which can otherwise fall through the grates, and benefits from the flavored wood. You actually end up baking the fish on a plank of wood, then lightly smoking it. You can buy planks at specialty-food stores or online, in cedar, white oak, hickory, and other wood varieties.

One of my favorite new devices is a silicone grilling mat, which I use mostly for grilling fish. This was popularized in the kitchen by Martha Stewart, but it's found a great place on the grill. You put it on the cooking grate, not directly on the briquettes or flavor bars. When it's greased with a little oil, fish won't stick or burn.

The whole key is bringing the food to finale by finishing it correctly. People tend to get very impatient cooking food on the grill. It's a great temptation to lift that hood, but every time you do you'll lose 200 degrees and add time to the cooking. Everybody's got a friend who gets antsy and wants to look at the food every five seconds. Here's a way to get your guests to cooperate, by asking, "Are you hungry? Then lift the hood and wait another half hour."

HEALTHY GRILLING

A lot of people like the charcoal flavor but they've read government health warnings about carcinogens in the food. Here are some ways to have a healthier grill experience. One way to reduce risk, especially with poultry, is to use brine, that is, a solution of water with either just salt, salt and sugar, or salt and various spices. The longer you cook on the grill the more you're going to alter the food, and the goal is to serve the food to the liking of your taste and the liking of your tenderness, without turning it into a piece of shoe leather.

If you've ever had kosher chicken, you know they're some of the best-tasting chickens you could possibly have. They're soaked in the brine, which leaves behind a layer of salt, holding the moisture into the chicken, so it makes for some very tasty poultry. Executive chef Dana M. Smith of Bobby Q's Barbecue and

Grill in Westport, Connecticut, smokes a boned turkey every Thanksgiving that's netted to hold it together. He uses two full breasts wrapped in a net similar to cheesecloth, which you can pick up at a chef's specialty store or on the Internet. Everything is brined overnight with a salt and pickling solution. In a five-gallon bucket he submerges a 7- to 9-pound turkey, soaks it overnight with half a cup of salt and some pickling spice, then lets it go 24 hours. He takes it out of the water, lets it dry out a little bit, puts some rub in it, and then it gets smoked for five to seven hours at about 250 degrees. If you have the ability to do home smoking, you can do it at a little lower temperature. Let it sit for about 15 or 20 minutes, then slice it up.

Marinades can also help to reduce health risks. The American Institute for Cancer Research says that even briefly marinating foods can reduce the amount of cancer-causing compounds from 92 to 99 percent.

The best way to marinate something is to actually perforate the food, so it sucks up the marinade like a sponge. Just scoring a piece of beef with a fork may not be enough. Consider doing what commercial chefs do, using a meat tenderizer tool like a Jaccard. It's got 48 stainless-steel saber blades in it. If a cut of beef has got a little sinew, the blades come down through and perforate the meat.

Use the Jaccard, for example, on London broil, which should be marinated overnight, up to 24 hours. For ribs, marinate overnight and put them in the fridge. Use something acidic in your marinade—vinegar, red wine, white wine, lemon juice, or orange juice, which can break down the tendons and make the ribs tender.

A brisket can be prepared with a wet rub, made with brown or white sugar, and when it cooks it creates a nice "bark," a caramelized crust that keeps the juices inside. Be careful of overmarinating the brisket, however, because it could make the meat break down before it's cooked. Under an hour is best.

A beer can is a great tool for cooking poultry by placing the can in the crevice of the bird. Use a roasting chicken and a can of Foster's, pour half of it out onto the chicken and rub all over, then put the beer can in the chicken's cavity. The can will help the heat generate more equally, and with the beer coming out, it will give the chicken more plumpness. What you want to do is crisp the skin, seal it, then slow-cook the chicken. If you cook on high heat in the first part of the cooking, you don't need to turn it up at the end.

Fishermen and outdoorsmen have long used buttermilk to marinate fresh fish. Buttermilk takes all the oil out of the fish, which is one of the biggest issues with cooking even the freshest of catches. While you shouldn't soak fish longer than 30 minutes with a conventional marinade, as it may get soggy, you could soak fish in buttermilk for a couple of hours. If the fish is good and chilled, it shouldn't be a problem. You can add some spices and put the fish in a resealable food storage bag.

Salmon is a great fish to cook on the grill. Problem is, when people cook a salmon on the grill, they do it with the skin down. There's oil between the skin and the fillet, so the skin is going to get stuck, and all the oil is being cooked up through the fillet, which gives it a fishy taste. If you cook it on a plank, it's not going to boil all the skin into the food, so the salmon will have a better, more distinctive taste. To cook bluefish, take all the skin off the back and remove all the oil.

One way to prepare the fish is to bake the fish on the grill in aluminum foil. Use a thermometer and wait

BIG DADDY LOWDOWN

Hybrid Grills Come of Age

The best of all possible grills? Some models now on the market combine gas and charcoal grills in one unit. Many are made of stainless steel, making them durable and easy to maintain.

until it's reached the desired temperature. It will come off the grill flaky, delicious, and ready to eat.

THE NEXT STEP

Chicken, fish, and beef are only the start of the holiday grilling experience. It's good to have something on the side. Side dishes can complement or complete the meal, so grill away and be creative. Jumbo shrimp or large scallops, bell peppers, asparagus, mushrooms (shiitake, morel, portobello, crimini), potatoes, lobster tails, polenta, onions, zucchini, corn on the cob, eggplant, Swiss chard, and baby carrots are just a few of your options.

Have faith and confidence in your grilling skill and personal style. And remember, before you get started, these keys to success:

- Pay attention to what's on the grill.
- Know how to judge how long something is cooking.
- Don't keep looking every five seconds—the watched pot never boils.
- Be patient. Grilling can be a long process. If it takes a turkey four hours, people say, "How can you be patient for that long?" I say I find something else to do! Some of the best meats you'll ever taste sit in a smoker overnight before they're ready, but I guarantee you'll be glad you waited when you pull that sucker off and get ready to chow down.

Holidays are important times in our lives, and you want to serve a great meal every time. So remember, even though you may be outside with a beer and a Frisbee, whether it's ninety degrees on Christmas morning and you're surrounded by palm trees, or it's ten below and the charcoal fire is all that's keeping you warm, grilling is like baking: it's precise, it's timing, and it's follow-through. That's follow-through the whole way through, not just at the beginning with your marinade, not just halfway through with good grilling sense, but paying attention at every step of the way to make sure you're going to have food come off the fire that's worthwhile eating, and good enough to keep you outside all year-round!

BIG DADDY LOWDOWN

Grill Basics

Be sure the grill is sturdy and well made. Ideally, it should provide areas of both direct and indirect heat. The cooking surface should be large enough to allow you to grill several portions of food at once, so you won't have to keep too many hungry guests waiting too long.

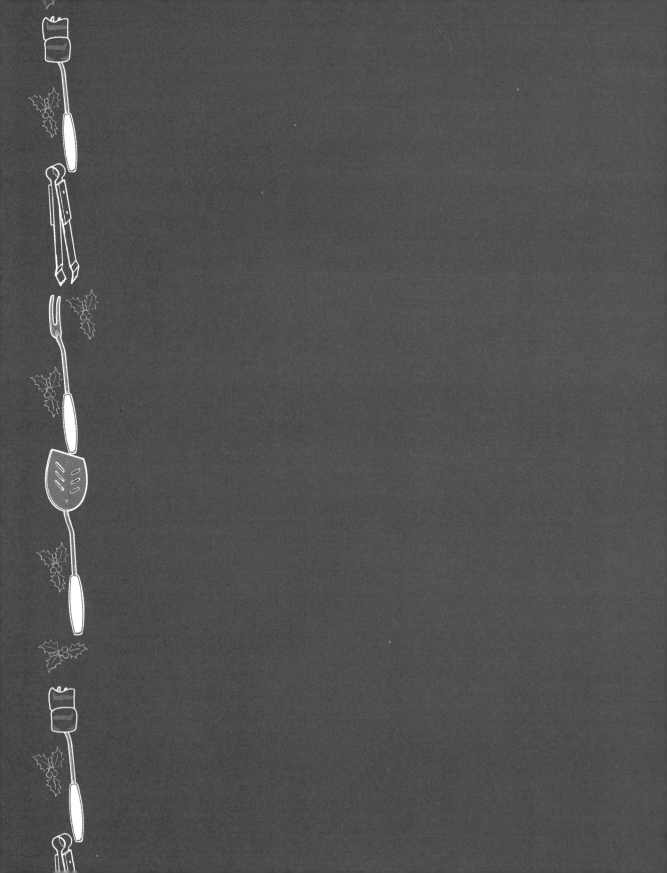

Chapter 2

Thanksgiving Feasts

Thanksgiving is the holiday that brings people together. Whether little kids and grandparents or college kids are coming home from around the country, it's a big scene around the dinner table—turkey, cranberry sauce, the works. How many of you are sick of the dried-out turkey that's been stuck trussed in the oven for five hours? Or the half-rare turkey that is just this side of inedible because it's been undercooked at the last minute? With all those people there, the world is counting on you. Don't mess it up with an inferior meal. The new trend is to take the turkey outdoors—just as our forefathers did. Having a turkey on the grill is an exciting and fun way to bring the family together, even if it is just getting a wee bit nippy out there. And you can still run in from time to time and find out what the Detroit Lions are doing in their annual football fest.

The first Thanksgiving feast served many different kinds of wild birds. The feast went on for days. Now, it is down to one long weekend. Turkey, of course, is the main staple, but other types of poultry are now common in

many Thanksgiving feasts. The Indians even brought popcorn to the feast. It was a big hit, unheard of before this date by Europeans. I recommend wrapping a turkey in foil, cooking it on the grill to temperature, then removing the foil for the last 30 minutes to give it a glazed, golden brown outer skin. When your family and friends gather around the table they'll tell you this is the best turkey they've ever eaten.

Some experts prefer to cook their bird in the Egg, an oblong smoker. Our friend Jim did a 12-pound turkey breast on the Egg over Thanksgiving, and it was moister than the one that came out of the oven. No basting. Never lifted the hood the whole time. "I had my probe thermometer, so I knew what the inside was doing, and I had the outside temperature gauge, so I knew what the outside was doing," Jim says. "I knew that the temperature was no more than 300 degrees."

Along with turkey, we'll show you some special variations on a holiday feast, including sides of Grill-Roasted Apples and Cheddar Appetizers, Creamy Pumpkin Soup, Yam or Sweet Potato Soufflé, Old-Fashioned Creamed Spinach, Cranberry-Mango Salsa, Dried-Cherry Stuffing, Corn Bread, Herb, and Apple Stuffing—and to top it off, Pecan Pie. Then, just when you thought couldn't eat another bite, we're going to whip out the big guns by letting our good friend Budha Mangus share his Triple-Stuffed Turducken spread.

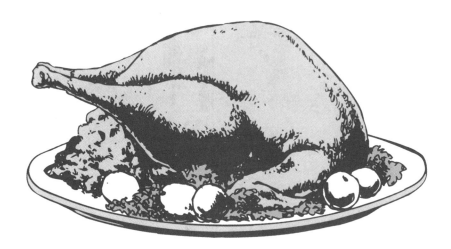

BBQ Turkey Legs, Thighs, and Drumsticks

3 or 4 turkey legs, thighs
attached, rinsed and
patted dry on paper
towels (figure on 3
pounds for 6 hungry
people and 4 pounds
for 8 big eaters)

1 teaspoon sea salt

4 cloves garlic, minced

4 tablespoons minced
parsley or cilantro

1 stick butter, at room
temperature

½ teaspoon cayenne pepper

½ teaspoon freshly ground
black pepper

Juice of 1 lemon

1 cup barbecue sauce (your
own or your favorite from
a bottle)

This requires long, slow cooking, but by using just the whole legs, it's faster than smoking the whole turkey.

Serves 6 to 8

Prepare the coals and make sure they are low and white-hot. Position the rack 8 inches above the coals. Or set your gas grill on medium.

Lay the turkey legs out on a work surface and sprinkle with sea salt.

In a small bowl, blend the garlic and parsley (or cilantro) into the softened butter. Add the two kinds of pepper.

BIG DADDY LOWDOWN

How Much Sauce Is Just Right?

If the condiment is intensely flavored, allow 2 to 3 tablespoons for each serving. For a less intense flavor, count on serving about ⅓ cup to each person.

Tease the butter mixture under the turkey skin and rub it into the outside of the legs.

Place the turkey legs on the grill and close the lid.

Grill-roast the turkey legs for 20 minutes on each side.

Mix the lemon juice with the barbecue sauce and paint the turkey legs with sauce.

Make sure the turkey is 150 degrees at its thickest part.

Serve with extra barbecue sauce on the side.

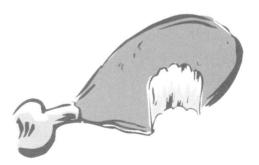

Grilled, Stuffed Boneless Turkey Breast

Stuffing:

2 cups corn bread stuffing

1 stick butter, melted

1 bunch chives, minced

2 teaspoons dried thyme
  leaves

½ cup chicken broth, or as
  needed

2 boxes frozen creamed
  spinach, defrosted

8 ounces ricotta cheese

2 tablespoons grated
  Parmesan cheese

2 ounces prosciutto ham

To assemble:

3 pounds boneless, skinless
  turkey breast in one large
  piece (about one half of a
  good-sized turkey breast)

Salt and pepper to taste

8 fresh sage leaves

¼ cup olive oil

This is very pretty when you slice across the rolled turkey breast. The more fillings you add, the prettier the dish. Use packaged turkey gravy and make the turkey roll the night before!

Serves 6

Mix the corn bread stuffing, butter, chives, and thyme. Add the chicken broth and mix well.

Open the boxes of defrosted creamed spinach and the ricotta.

Lay the turkey breast on a piece of waxed paper.

Place a second piece of waxed paper on top to cover.

Pound the daylights out of it with a mallet or 5-pound barbell until the meat is very flat and large.

Sprinkle lightly with salt and pepper. On the long side nearest you, arrange the fresh sage leaves. Spread the stuffing, ¼ inch thick, over the turkey, pressing it into the flesh.

Spoon on the creamed spinach, very carefully, pressing it down and spreading it with the back of your spoon. Spoon the ricotta over the top, then sprinkle with the Parmesan cheese. Gently press the filling down with the flat of your hand. Arrange the prosciutto on top. Starting with the long side nearest to you, carefully roll the turkey breast into a very fat sausage. Tie with kitchen string, not too tightly, but firmly. Wrap in aluminum foil. At this point, you can place the roll in the refrigerator. Remove from the fridge an hour before cooking.

Remove the foil. Sprinkle the roll with salt and pepper and rub with olive oil. Roast over slow coals, or in a 350-degree gas grill for 1 hour, turning occasionally. The internal temperature should be about 150 degrees. When done, let the roll rest for 10 minutes. Slice carefully and see the beautiful colored wheels! You can serve it with Alfredo sauce or turkey gravy.

Smoked Turkey

10- to 12-pound turkey,
   brined for 24 hours
   (soaked in water, spices,
   and salt)
Juice of one lemon
Dried sage leaves
½ cup peanut oil
Salt and freshly ground
   black pepper

This is a delicious way to prepare your turkey. It's even better if you brine the turkey for 24 hours before smoking. If you don't have a smoker, you can use your grill. Have plenty of chips (hickory or apple are great smoker chips) on hand that you have presoaked.

Serves 15 to 18

Start soaking your wood chips the night before. Get your smoker or your grill ready. It should not be terribly hot, or set your gas grill at 300 degrees.

Pat the turkey dry. Sprinkle it with the lemon juice inside and out. Mix the sage leaves with the peanut oil and rub on the bird, then dust with salt and pepper.

Smoke the turkey for 5 to 6 hours, turning every 20 minutes. If you have a rotisserie in your grill or smoker, so much the better.

When the turkey is 155 degrees at its thickest part, like the thigh, place it on a platter and let it rest for 20 minutes, so when you carve it, the juices won't run out.

Serve with packaged gravy, relish, chutney, or your favorite watermelon pickle on the side.

Note: The giblets make great stock for gravy, especially if you add the wing tips!

MINI-FEAST
Rock Cornish Game Hens—
Stuffed and Grill-Roasted

Dried-Cherry Stuffing (see
   page 31)
2 game hens—they come in
   two sizes, 8 to 10 ounces
   and 1½ pounds; either is
   just fine, rinsed in cold
   water and patted dry,
   wings and giblets
   removed for stock
Two 4-inch sprigs fresh
   rosemary
Salt and freshly ground
   black pepper to taste

Basting sauce:

2 tablespoons butter
2 tablespoon dry white wine
2 cloves garlic, minced
½ teaspoon dry English
   mustard

So this year, the kids are gone and it's just you and your main squeeze. Or you are just starting out—no kids yet and parents nowhere to be found. This recipe is easily doubled if you decide to have friends in and share.

Serves 2

You can make the stuffing the day before and refrigerate it, just don't stuff the birds until the last moment.

Prepare your grill at 350 degrees. Place a sprig of rosemary inside the cavity of each game hen. Sprinkle with salt and freshly ground black pepper. Stuff the birds by placing about ½ cup of the stuffing in each. Skewer the ends closed. Bake the rest of the stuffing in a dish, in the oven or on the grill.

In a small pot, mix all of the basting sauce ingredients together, melt, and keep warm.

Place the birds on the grill and baste frequently. Roast for 30 minutes, turning every time you baste. Let rest for 10 minutes before serving.

ELEGANT THANKSGIVING
Bacon-Wrapped Roast Pheasants

2 pheasants, rinsed and
   patted dry
6 slices bacon
½ cup apricot jam, heated to
   liquefy

Rub:
½ stick butter, at room
   temperature
1 tablespoon peanut oil
1 tablespoon paprika
1 teaspoon garlic powder
½ teaspoon hot red pepper
   sauce

Two pheasants make a perfect dinner for six light eaters or four big appetites. Pheasants are very lean and can easily dry out. Tie on the bacon after giving them a good rub as directed. They are tender and delicious if not overcooked.

Serves 4 to 6

Mix the ingredients for the rub in a bowl.

Rub them all over the outside and insides of the pheasants. Stretch out the bacon strips and secure them to the pheasants with toothpicks. Grill the pheasants over moderate flame, at about 300 degrees for 30 minutes. Turn frequently.

When the bacon starts to burn, remove it and brush the pieces of pheasant with hot apricot jam.

Let caramelize for two to three minutes, plate, and serve. Do not overcook, or the pheasant will dry out.

Roast Ducks with Dried-Cherry Stuffing

Dried-Cherry Stuffing (see page 31)

To precook the ducks:
2 large ducklings, about 5 pounds each
4 bay leaves
2 lemons, cut in quarters
1 tablespoon salt
4 tablespoons Worcestershire sauce
2 tablespoons hot red pepper sauce (such as Tabasco)
1 cup apple cider vinegar

Basting sauce:
1 cup dry white wine
1 cup cherry jam, heated and strained
¼ cup Worcestershire sauce

This is an easy way to ensure that your duck is both tender on the inside and crisply delicious on the outside. You can make the Dried-Cherry Stuffing well in advance and freeze or refrigerate it. Just don't prestuff the ducks, as you will be boiling them prior to grilling them.

Serves 8

You can make the stuffing the day before and refrigerate it, just don't stuff the birds until the last moment.

Rinse the ducklings, pat dry with paper towels, and set them aside.

Mix the rest of the ingredients in a large stockpot and put in the ducks.

Cover with cold water and bring to a boil (this will release most of the fat that is under the skin). Reduce heat, and simmer the ducks for 20 minutes.

Remove the ducks from the pot and drain off the liquid. Do not reserve the liquid. Stuff the ducks and tie the legs together.

Set your grill at 400 degrees. Brown the ducks all over, turning frequently. Lower the heat to 300 degrees, prick the ducks with a fork to release fat, close the lid, and roast for another 20 minutes, basting and turning often to coat with the sauce.

Be sure to have an ovenproof casserole dish with lots of extra stuffing on the side.

Let rest 10 to 15 minutes before carving.

Southwest Rubbed Turkey with Skin Filled with Peppers and Corn Bread

Filling:

1 stick butter or margarine, at room temperature

1 cup commercial corn bread stuffing

2 to 4 canned chipotle peppers, minced

¼ cup roasted red peppers, skin removed, chopped

1 bunch fresh chives

2 cloves garlic

Rub:

2 tablespoons Hungarian paprika (not sweet)

2 tablespoons dried sage leaves (not powdered)

2 tablespoons coarse salt, either sea salt or kosher

2 tablespoons ground black pepper

Basting sauce:

1 cup dry white wine

2 sticks butter

¼ cup Worcestershire sauce

Juice of ½ lemon

It's amazing how much flavorful filling you can tease between a turkey skin and flesh. You just have to be very careful not to break the skin. You can push the filling from one side of the breast down into the thigh and drumstick! It may look a bit lumpy and funny before you roast it, but no one will notice when the bird is brown and all that filling has given it enormous flavor!

Serves 10 to 16, depending on size of people, their appetites, and what else you are serving as sides

Blend all the filling ingredients in the bowl of your food processor and set aside.

Mix all the rub ingredients well in a small bowl and set aside.

Put all the basting sauce ingredients in a small saucepan and heat until the butter melts; keep warm but do not boil.

To assemble for roasting: Take a 14- to 16-pound turkey, rinsed in cold water and patted dry with paper towels. If the turkey isn't icy cold, the skin will be more pliable to tease in the filling.

Start putting bits (about a teaspoon at a time) of filling between the skin and the flesh, starting with the breast and gently pushing it into the thigh, then the drumstick.

When you've completely filled the area between the skin and flesh, rub the turkey with the rub, working it into the skin.

Set your grill at 250 degrees, or build a fire with briquettes that are hot but not flaming.

Wrap the turkey in aluminum foil and roast for 3 hours. Remove the foil, baste, and roast for another 3 to 4 hours, basting frequently. Remove from the grill when the turkey reaches 140-degree internal temperature, and let it rest, covered with a clean kitchen towel, for 15 minutes. The turkey will continue to cook as it rests.

If you roast the turkey in your indoor oven, be sure to use the drippings to make a spicy gravy.

BIG DADDY LOWDOWN

The Joys of Bamboo

Use a bamboo cutting board for preparing your food—it won't take on water or food residue.

THANKSGIVING SIDES
Grill-Roasted Apple and Cheddar Appetizers

6 Granny Smith apples,
  peeled, cored, and cut
  horizontally into ¼- to
  ⅓-inch rounds

1 large baguette (sourdough,
  if you can find one)

Olive oil in a spray bottle

4 ounces sharp cheddar
  cheese, grated

Red pepper flakes, optional

This smells and tastes of fall. It's easy and wonderful!

Serves 8 to 10, depending on quantity and richness of your other hors d'oeuvres

Place the apple slices on a hot grill. Turn after 1 minute and grill for another minute.

Slice the baguette thin, spray both sides with the olive oil, and toast on one side. Turn and place the apple slices to cover the bread. Mound the cheese and bake until the cheese melts.

Sprinkle with hot red pepper flakes, if desired.

Creamy Pumpkin Soup

1 stick unsalted butter

2 tablespoons Wondra
quick-blending flour

1 medium yellow onion, cut
in small dice

2 cups rich chicken broth,
your own, or canned is
fine

13-ounce can pumpkin puree

½ teaspoon ground cinnamon

½ teaspoon ground allspice

1 tablespoon light brown
sugar, optional

2 cups heavy or whipping
cream

Salt and freshly ground
black pepper to taste

Pumpkin seeds or corn
bread croutons, for
garnish

Everyone loves this soup! It can be made in advance, and you can double the recipe easily. Just heat at the last minute and enjoy!

Serves 6

Melt the butter and add the flour, cooking over low heat until well blended. Add the onion and cook until softened, stirring constantly. Do not brown!

Add the chicken broth, pumpkin, and spices. Bring to a boil. In your blender, whirl the soup in batches, being careful not to overfill, returning smoothed soup to the pot.

At this point, you can refrigerate the soup until 30 minutes before serving. Reheat the soup. Add the cream and warm without boiling.

Serve in warm bowls or mugs, preferably outdoors while waiting for the bird to finish!

Sprinkle with a few pumpkin seeds or croutons floating on top.

Yam or Sweet Potato Soufflé

4 yams or sweet potatoes,
   fire roasted, skin on
½ stick unsalted butter
2 tablespoons all-purpose
   flour
2 shallots, peeled and
   minced
5 extra-large eggs,
   separated
2 teaspoons double-acting
   baking powder
¼ teaspoon ground allspice
¼ teaspoon ground nutmeg
2 tablespoons brown sugar
1 teaspoon salt
1 teaspoon cayenne pepper
Salt and pepper to taste
1 cup heavy or whipping
   cream, whipped
Toasted pecans or walnuts,
   for garnish

Okay, it's sweet, but that's fine on T-day! You could make it savory, but why? Just enjoy—let the soufflé puff in the oven while you are serving the turkey, bring this out as a side dish, and listen to the oohs and aahs.

Serves 6 to 8

Roast the potatoes for about 40 minutes; when a fork goes in easily, they are done. Cool and then remove the meat from the sweet potato or yams, dropping spoonfuls in the jar of your blender. You should have about 2 cups of pulp.

Melt the butter and add the flour and shallots. Stir until the flour is smooth and the shallots softened. Add to your blender.

Separate the eggs and set the whites aside in an immaculately clean bowl. Add the yolks to your blender. Whirl until smooth. Add the baking powder, allspice, nutmeg, sugar, salt, and cayenne pepper. Blend until very smooth.

Whip the egg whites until stiff peaks form. Whip the cream until stiff in another bowl.

Set your oven at 400 degrees. Prepare a 2-quart soufflé dish or deep baking dish with non-stick, butter-flavored spray.

Place the pureed yams in a big bowl. Add salt and pepper to taste. Gently fold in the egg whites. Fold in the whipped cream. Pour into the prepared soufflé dish or baking dish.

Bake for 40 to 45 minutes, or until the soufflé is puffed and well browned. Sprinkle with the toasted nuts and serve with turkey, duck, or whatever, and fixin's.

BIG DADDY LOWDOWN

Potato Placement

When cooking potatoes, place them around the edge of a covered grill and cook for 1½ hours before cooking steaks.

Old-Fashioned Creamed Spinach

1½ cups heavy or whipping
cream

2 shallots, minced

1 tablespoon Wondra quick-
blending flour

4 bags fresh baby spinach, or
4 boxes frozen chopped
spinach, thawed and
squeezed of excess water

1 teaspoon Worcestershire
sauce

¼ teaspoon ground nutmeg

Juice of 1 lemon

Zest of ½ lemon

Salt and pepper to taste

½ cup toasted bread crumbs,
for garnish

This is a traditional side dish, and, of course, you can get frozen creamed spinach, but don't! This recipe is a snap and everyone will love it. As much as it's old-fashioned, you don't have to chill your fingers or spend an hour washing spinach. Just get the baby spinach in the bag and go to town!

Serves 6 to 8

Bring the cream to a boil, let thicken, and add the shallots. Whisk in the flour.

Add the spinach and stir. Cook, letting the juices release. Turn burner to low and then let the mixture thicken, stirring constantly. Add the rest of the ingredients.

Place in a warm serving bowl. Garnish with the toasted bread crumbs.

Cranberry-Mango Salsa

1 bag cranberries, rinsed, picked over, stems removed

2 firm, ripe mangoes, peeled and cubed

1 cup white sugar (more if you've got a sweet tooth)

Juice of 1 lime

¼ cup orange juice

1 tablespoon orange zest

This is excellent with any form of poultry as well as pork.

Makes 2 cups

This is best made 2 days in advance.

In your food processor, pulse the cranberries until coarsely ground. Place them in a bowl.

Add the rest of the ingredients and stir to blend. Cover and refrigerate. Serve at room temperature.

Dried-Cherry Stuffing

6-ounce bag dried cherries

1 cup white wine or water, warmed

1 stick unsalted butter

1 cup finely chopped sweet white onion

2 stalks celery, with tops, finely chopped

10 fresh sage leaves, chopped

2 tablespoons fresh rosemary leaves, removed from stems

1 teaspoon dried thyme leaves

1 cup walnuts, toasted

1 loaf good white bread, cubed, or 5 cups dry stuffing

(If you are using the dried stuffing, you will need 1 cup chicken broth.)

½ cup chopped Italian flat-leaf parsley

Salt and freshly ground black pepper to taste

This is very good in turkey, chicken, or duck. It's also wonderful with pork, such as a filling for crown roast. Make plenty of extra so that you can have some on the side.

Makes 6 cups

Soak the cherries in the warm wine or water to reconstitute.

Melt the butter and add the onion and celery. Sauté until vegetables are soft. Add the herbs. Place with the rest of the ingredients in a large bowl, adding the cherries and any liquid. Mix so there is some integrity to the bread—mushy stuffing is less appealing.

You can stuff this into a bird, or bake it for 20 minutes to serve on the side.

Corn Bread, Herb, and Apple Stuffing

1 stick unsalted butter

4 stalks celery, tops on, chopped

1 cup chopped sweet onion

½ cup chopped fennel bulb

3 Granny Smith apples, peeled, cored, and chopped

1 tablespoon dried thyme leaves

Juice of 1 lemon

1 cup pecans, chopped and toasted

4 cups corn bread stuffing, packaged is fine

1 cup oysters, drained and chopped

1 cup chicken broth

This is another really traditional poultry stuffing, and you can add a cup of small shucked oysters, whole or cut in half. For years we made our own corn bread, then we tried the store-bought packages and they are just fine. The result is delectable!

Makes 6 cups

In a large frying pan, melt the butter and add the celery, sweet onion, and fennel. Sauté until the vegetables are soft.

Add the apples and sprinkle with the thyme and lemon juice.

Combine all of the ingredients in a large bowl, mixing well. Mix in 1 cup chicken broth. You can add more broth if the stuffing is very dry.

When you bake the stuffing on the side, it's nice to add some of the basting juices that you're using on the bird.

Pecan Pie

Dough for a 1-crust pie, your
   own, refrigerated, or
   frozen
1 stick unsalted butter
3 tablespoons all-purpose
   flour or Wondra quick-
   blending flour
4 extra-large eggs
1½ cups dark corn syrup
1 teaspoon vanilla extract
1 teaspoon salt
1½ cups pecans, halved, not
   chopped

This recipe is at least 75 years old and we got it from a good ole Southern gal 30 years ago who said it was her grandma's recipe—go figure! The best piecrust is homemade. Some of us are good at it, others are not. The recipe on the Crisco tub is one of the best, and you should make the dough the day before. Being one who is pie-dough challenged, I get the refrigerated dough, put it in a really nice pie dish, and it's almost as good!

A 10-inch pie should serve 6 to 8, depending on how big your guests' appetites are and what other desserts are on the table.

Set your oven at 425 degrees.

Spray a nice glass 10-inch pie plate with non-stick spray. Line it with pie dough and decoratively crimp the outside edges.

Melt the butter over low heat and mix in the flour, cooking until smooth and the flour gets rid of that "floury" taste. Do not brown. Set aside to cool.

Process the eggs in the jar of your blender and

slowly add the corn syrup. Add the vanilla and salt. With the motor running on low, pour in the butter mixture.

Pour into prepared pie plate and sprinkle with nuts. Bake at 425 degrees for 15 minutes. Reduce heat and bake for another 40 minutes at 325 degrees.

Serve with whipped cream, vanilla ice cream, or butter pecan ice cream.

A VERY BUDHA THANKSGIVING

We met Budha Mangus, aka Rick Stofer, back when we were preparing our first Big Daddy project—a kit with a cookbook, apron, and other goodies appropriately titled *Big Daddy's Zubba Bubba BBQ*. The next dozen or so recipes are all his and make up his full table spread. Check out the attached DVD to watch him prepare each of them, and look for more Budha recipes on www.budhamangus.com.

Budha's All-Purpose Rub

¾ cup coarse sea salt

1 ½ cups packed brown
   sugar

1 ½ cups white sugar

2 tablespoons ground cumin

2 tablespoons chili powder

2 tablespoons Hungarian
   paprika

2 tablespoons gourmet garlic
   powder

2 teaspoons black pepper

2 teaspoons cayenne pepper

2 teaspoons ground celery
   seed

1 teaspoon anise

1 teaspoon ground coriander

1 teaspoon Chinese five-
   spice powder

1 teaspoon Mexican oregano

1 tablespoon MSG (optional)

Budha's rub recipe is not only the corner-stone for much of the Thanksgiving feast that he has prepared for us, it's also a darn good rub, great for whatever meat you're preparing (hence the "All-Purpose").

Makes 4 ¹/₂ cups

Combine all the ingredients in a glass or plastic bowl. Unused mixture can be stored in an airtight container.

Smoked Garlic Puree

3 heads of garlic

3 tablespoons margarine

2 tablespoons olive oil (use
    as needed)

Enough of the recipes that follow call for smoked garlic, which adds a mellow, smoky barbecue flavor whenever it's added and can be used in any recipe requiring garlic. You can also remove the skin from the garlic prior to smoking if you prefer.

Makes approximately ¼ cup

Chop the top off the garlic heads to expose the garlic.

Top the garlic with the margarine and place on a piece of aluminum foil, tops up, in a 325-degree smoker. Smoke for 35 to 45 minutes, or until the garlic is soft.

Allow the garlic to cool and gently separate the cloves, then peel by squeezing, and drop into your food processor. It is important that no skin or hard areas are included in the mixture.

Process until a fine puree is created, adding the olive oil as needed.

Budha's Margarita-Stuffed Jalapeños and Mushrooms

18 whole jalapeño peppers

1 cup tequila

¼ cup Triple Sec

Juice from 3 medium limes

18 medium white mushrooms

3 tablespoons margarine

2 tablespoons minced onion

2 tablespoons Smoked Garlic Puree (see page 37)

12 ounces cream cheese

2 tablespoons Dijon-style mustard

¼ cup chopped cilantro

Zest of 1 lime

1 tablespoon prepared horseradish

6 ounces crabmeat

¼ cup chopped water chestnuts

4 tablespoons grated Parmesan cheese

2 tablespoons Budha's All-Purpose Rub (see page 36)

Serves 12

Cut the caps and stems off the jalapeños, and reserve the caps.

Using your potato peeler, core the jalapeño peppers and remove the seeds and the membrane. Rinse in cold water. Coring the peppers will help to lower the level of capsaicin (the chemical in peppers that makes them hot).

With a toothpick push a small hole in the bottom of the peppers to allow liquids to seep through.

Place the jalapeños, reserved caps, tequila, Triple Sec, and juice from 2 limes in a nonreactive container. Cover and refrigerate overnight. (Wash your hands before touching sensitive areas of the body!)

Remove the jalapeños and caps from tequila mixture and allow peppers to drain. (You can retain the tequila mixture for some powerful shots later on!)

Remove stems from the mushrooms, retaining both stems and caps, and chop the stems finely, along with the jalapeño caps.

In a medium saucepan, melt the margarine. Brush the mushroom caps with margarine. In the remaining margarine sauté the mushroom stems, jalapeño caps, onion, and garlic puree until the onions are tender. Remove from heat.

In a separate bowl, combine cream cheese, mustard, cilantro, lime zest, and horseradish. Stir until smooth. Add the juice of 1 lime to the mixture, along with the crabmeat and water chestnuts. Scoop mixture into a resealable plastic bag and cut off the bag's corner, then pipe the mixture into the mushroom caps and jalapeño shells. Push a toothpick into jalapeños, about halfway up.

Place the jalapeños in jalapeño cooking rack and the mushrooms in a shallow aluminum foil pan. Smoke at 230 to 250 degrees for about 1 hour. Remove from smoker. Garnish with Parmesan cheese, cilantro, and Budha's All-Purpose Rub and serve.

Triple-Stuffed Turducken

1 cup Budha's All-Purpose
    Rub (see page 36)
Andouille Sausage Dressing
    (recipe follows)
Seafood Dressing (recipe
    follows)
Sage Dressing (recipe
    follows)
Cajun Basting Sauce (recipe
    follows)
12- to 15-pound turkey
4- to 6-pound duck
3- to 5-pound chicken

Serves 10 to 15

Prepare the dressings and basting sauce per recipes below and refrigerate until needed while you prep your poultry. Remember when handling poultry to follow food-handling guidelines. Keep the poultry below 40 degrees and sanitize all surfaces.

2 sticks margarine

7 cups chopped onion

3 cups chopped celery

3 cups chopped green bell
  pepper

2 lbs. chopped andouille
  sausage

3 tablespoons Smoked
  Garlic Puree (see page
  37)

¼ cup Budha's All-Purpose
  Rub (see page 36)

2 tablespoons Frank's Red
  Hot Sauce

1 teaspoon salt

1 teaspoon pepper

2 cups chicken broth, to add
  moisture as needed

3 to 5 cups dried bread
  cubes

2 eggs

Andouille Sausage Dressing

Makes 8 cups

In an 8-quart saucepan, melt 1 stick of margarine. Add 3½ cups chopped onion, 1½ cups chopped celery, and 1½ cups green pepper. Sauté until the celery is tender, stirring and scraping often.

Add the sausage and cook until sausage is well browned, stirring often.

Stir in 1 stick margarine, and then add the rest of the onion, celery, and green pepper, along with the garlic puree, rub, hot sauce, and salt and pepper. Stir well, cooking until the vegetables are crisp-tender.

Stir in the stock and bring to boil, and cook until the fat rises to the top and coats the surface. Reduce the heat to low and stir in 4 cups of bread cubes and the eggs. Mix well. Continue adding the bread cubes as needed to form stiff stuffing.

Allow the stuffing to cool completely and refrigerate until ready to stuff the birds.

1½ cups chopped onion

1½ cups chopped celery

1½ cups chopped green bell
   pepper

1½ sticks margarine

6 ounces shrimp

6 ounces crawfish

6 ounces crabmeat

1 teaspoon Smoked Garlic
   Puree (see page 37)

3 bay leaves

¼ cup chopped green onion

½ cup Budha's All-Purpose
   Rub (see page 36)

1 egg

1 cup Italian bread crumbs

1 cup chicken broth, to add
   moisture as needed

Seafood Dressing

Makes 3 cups

Sauté ¾ cup onion, ¾ cup celery, and ¾ cup green pepper with 6 tablespoons of the margarine until the vegetables start to wilt.

Add the shrimp, crawfish, and crabmeat and sauté until the shrimp begins to turn orange.

Add the rest of the vegetables, the garlic puree, bay leaves, and green onion and the rest of the margarine.

Remove from the heat once margarine has melted. Add the rub, egg, and bread crumbs.

Mix completely. If dry, add broth as needed. Refrigerate.

½ cup chopped onion

½ cup chopped celery

½ cup chopped green bell
    pepper

½ stick margarine

¼ cup chopped cilantro

2 cups bread cubes

2 cups Pepperidge Farm
    stuffing

1 teaspoon pepper

2 eggs

½ teaspoon salt

¼ to ½ teaspoon rubbed sage

¼ to ½ teaspoon poultry
    seasoning

2 cups chicken broth, to add
    moisture as needed

Sage Dressing

Makes 6 cups

Sauté the onion, celery, and green pepper in the margarine until onions are softened.

Combine the sauteed vegetables with cilantro, bread, stuffing, pepper, eggs, salt, sage, and poultry seasoning in a large mixing bowl. Stir in the broth until well moistened. Refrigerate until needed.

2 sticks margarine

1 cup Frank's Red Hot Sauce

1 cup soy sauce

½ cup Worcestershire sauce

1 cup Gates Spicy BBQ
    sauce

¼ cup Budha's All-Purpose
    Rub (see page 36)

Cajun Basting Sauce

Makes 4 cups

Melt the margarine over medium heat and add the rest of the ingredients. Stir until all the ingredients are combined. The sauce can be used as a baste for any poultry, and will be injected into the turducken with a flavor injector.

BONE YOUR POULTRY

For the most part, boning is the same for all types of poultry. When you complete the process you will have a completely boned chicken or duck. For the turkey you will leave the tips of the legs and the first two joints of the wings. Start with the turkey, as it is larger and easier to work with. As you bone the birds be careful to avoid piercing the skin except for the initial cuts in the birds. Cuts in the skin will tend to expand during the cooking process, leading to drying of the meat.

For the Turkey: Place the bird, breast down, on a flat surface. Make an incision the entire length of the spine through the skin and flesh. Starting from the neck end and using the tip of the knife, follow as close to the bone as you can cut, carefully teasing the skin and meat away from the frame with blade and fingers. Toward the neck end, cut through the meat to expose the shoulder blade. Feel for it first and cut through small amounts of meat at a time if you have trouble locating it; cut the meat away from around the bone and sever the bone at the joint so you can remove the blade. Disjoint the wing between the second and third joints; free the heavy drumstick of the wing and remove it, being careful to leave the skin intact. Continue teasing the meat away from the backbone, heading toward the thighbone and being careful to keep the "oyster" (pocket of meat on the back) attached to the skin instead of leaving it with the bone.

Again, being careful not to break through the skin, use a small hammer to break the leg bone completely across, about two inches from the tip end. Then manipulate both ends of the bone with your hands to be sure the break is complete. Leave the tip of the bone in, but remove the leg bone and thighbone as one unit. To do this, cut the meat away from around the thighbone first, using the knife tip; then, holding the thighbone up with one hand, use the other hand to carefully cut the meat away from around the leg-thigh joint. (Don't cut through this joint, and don't worry if it seems as if you're leaving a lot of meat around the joint—it can't be helped and, besides, it will add flavor when you make the stock with the bones!) Then use the blade of the knife to scrape the meat away from the leg bone; remove the leg-thigh bone. With your hands or the knife, remove as many pin bones from the leg meat as possible; then, if necessary, pull the tip of the leg bone to turn the meat to the inside (so the skin is on the outside and it looks like a turkey again).

For the Duck and Chicken: Debone each wing, and cut off the first two joints of the wing, leaving the wing's drumstick; cut the meat from around the drumstick and remove this bone. When you reach the thigh, follow the thigh-leg bone with the knife blade to release the bone as one unit, again being careful not to cut through the skin.

Cut through the ball-and-socket joint to release the thighbone from the carcass; you should now be able to open up the bird more to better see what bones are still left to deal with. Continue teasing the meat away from the carcass until you reach the center front of the breastbone. Then very carefully separate the skin from the breastbone at the midline without piercing the skin (go slowly because the skin is very thin at this point). Repeat the same boning procedure on the other side (left or right) of the bird, with the breast down. When both sides are finished, carefully remove the carcass. Then remove the thighbone and leg bone on each side.

TO ASSEMBLE THE TURDUCKEN

Spread the turkey, skin down, on a flat surface exposing as much meat as possible. Sprinkle the meat generously and evenly with about 2 tablespoons of the Budha's All-Purpose Rub, patting it in with your hands. Ensure that you turn the leg, thigh, and wing meat to the outside so you can season it, too. Inject the turkey with the Cajun Basting Sauce. Stuff some of the cold Andouille

Sausage Dressing into the leg, thigh, and wing cavities until full but not tightly packed (if too tightly packed, it may cause the leg and wing to burst open during cooking). Spread an even layer of the dressing over the remaining exposed meat, about ½ to ¾ inch thick. You should use a total of about 7 cups dressing.

Place the duck, skin down, on top of the Andouille Sausage Dressing, arranging the duck evenly over the dressing. Season the exposed duck meat generously and evenly with about 1 tablespoon more of the Budha's All-Purpose Rub, pressing it in with your hands. Inject the duck with the Cajun Basting Sauce, then spread the Seafood Dressing evenly over the exposed duck meat, making the layer slightly less thick than that of the Andouille Sausage Dressing, about ½ inch thick. Use a total of about 4 cups dressing.

Arrange the chicken, skin down, evenly on top of the Seafood Dressing. Season the exposed chicken meat generously and evenly with about 1 tablespoon more of the Budha's All-Purpose Rub, pressing it in with your hands. Inject the chicken with the Cajun Basting Sauce. Spread the Sage Dressing evenly over the exposed chicken meat, using about 3 cups dressing and making the layer about ½ inch thick.

To finish off the Turducken you will need a helper. Have your helper hold the turkey closed while you sew up all openings, making the stitches about 1 inch apart; when you finish sewing up the Turducken on the first side, turn it over in the pan to sew closed any openings on the other side. Then tie the legs together just above the tip bones. Leave the Turducken breast side up in the pan, tucking in the turkey wings.

Place the Turducken pan in a slightly larger pan with sides at least 2½ inches deep, so that the larger pan will catch the overflow of drippings during cooking. Season the exposed side of the Turducken generously and evenly with about 2 tablespoons more of the Budha's All-Purpose Rub, patting it in with your hands. Refrigerate until ready to smoke.

Bring your smoker to 225 degrees to 250 degrees and place the bird on a center rack. Smoke until a meat thermometer inserted through to the center reads 180 degrees, approximately 7 to 10 hours. Starting at the 6-hour mark, begin mopping the bird with the Cajun Basting Sauce every 45 minutes.

When the Turducken registers 180 degrees, remove from smoker using strong tongs or spatulas inserted underneath (remember there are no bones to support the bird's structure), carefully transfer the Turducken to a serving platter, and present it to your guests before carving. Then place the Turducken on a flat surface to carve. Be sure to make your slices crosswise so that each slice contains all three dressings and all three meats. (It's easy to do this and still have manageable-size servings if you slice the Turducken in half lengthwise, then cut servings crosswise to the desired thickness from one side of the Turducken at a time.) Serve additional bowls of the dressings on the side.

Applejack Twice-Baked Sweet Potatoes

4 pounds sweet potatoes

Vegetable oil

¾ stick margarine

½ cup Jack Daniel's

¼ cup firmly packed light
   brown sugar

1 cup chopped apple

¼ cup apple-juice
   concentrate

¼ cup maple syrup

1 teaspoon salt

1 teaspoon ground cinnamon

½ teaspoon ground ginger

¼ teaspoon ground cloves

½ teaspoon allspice

2 cups miniature
   marshmallows (optional)

½ cup chopped pecans
   (optional)

Serves 6 to 8

Scrub the potatoes and oil them lightly. Prick the potatoes several times with the tines of a fork, then wrap in aluminum foil and place to the side of the hot charcoal in the smoker and bake for 30 to 45 minutes, or until tender when squeezed with an oven mitt. Rotate the potatoes about halfway through the cooking.

Remove the potatoes from the foil, cut them in half lengthwise, and scoop out the meat, leaving a thin shell of meat around the edges. Select 6 to 8 of the nicest shells and reserve for stuffing, discarding the excess shells. Mash the removed meat in a mixing bowl. Add 3 tablespoons of the margarine, the Jack Daniel's, and brown sugar. Set the mixture aside.

In a large skillet, melt the remaining 3 tablespoons margarine, add apples, and sauté for a few minutes. Add the apple juice concentrate, maple syrup, and spices to the apples and toss to mix. Combine the apple mixture with the potatoes and let cool.

Spoon the mixture into a large resealable plastic bag. Snip off a corner of the bag and pipe the mixture into the reserved shells, filling to above the edges of the shells. Place the potatoes in a foil pan in a single layer and top with the marshmallows and pecans, if desired. Potatoes can be covered with foil and refrigerated or frozen. Before serving, place in a 350-degree smoker or oven and bake for 25 to 30 minutes.

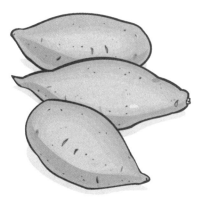

Grilled Corn on the Cob

8 ears of corn with husks

1 gallon cold water

1 cup white sugar

3 jalapeño peppers

1 stick margarine

1 tablespoon Smoked Garlic
  Puree (see page 37)

2 teaspoons salt

2 teaspoons pepper

Juice of 1 lime

Serves 8

Pull back the husks from corn and remove the silk.

In a large bucket, place water and sugar and mix until sugar has dissolved. Soak prepared corn in refrigerator for 1 hour.

Remove the seeds from the jalapeños and grill over a hot grill until the peppers are slightly charred. Remove from the grill and mince jalapeños. Melt the margarine and add the remaining ingredients. Remove from heat and allow mixture to cool.

Remove the corn from the water and coat the kernels with mixture. Reposition the husks to cover the kernels and tie with twine or pieces of husk. Position over medium-heat grill, turning the corn every 2 minutes. After a couple of turns of the corn, move the corn from direct heat to indirect heat. Continue to roast for 15 to 20 minutes. Serve corn hot off of the grill in full husk.

Budha's Broccoli Casserole

¼ cup chopped onion

¾ stick margarine

2 teaspoons all-purpose
    flour

½ cup water

8 ounces Velveeta cheese

2 ounces cream cheese

Two 10-ounce packages
    frozen chopped broccoli,
    thawed, excess water
    squeezed out

3 eggs

Oyster crackers

Serves 8

In a large pot placed on your grill or stovetop, at a medium heat, sauté the onion in margarine until semiclear. Stir in the flour and water and cook until thickened. Melt the cheeses and blend in the broccoli. Mix in the eggs and place mixture in a 9x13-inch greased aluminum pan and cover with oyster crackers. Place in 325- to 350-degree smoker or oven for 35 minutes.

Twice-Baked Garlic Potatoes

4 pounds potatoes

1 cup heavy or whipping
cream

½ cup sour cream

½ stick margarine

1 tablespoon Smoked Garlic
Puree (see page 37)

1 teaspoon salt

1 teaspoon pepper

1 cup fancy shredded
cheddar cheese

1 tablespoon Budha's All-
Purpose Rub (see page
36)

Serves 6 to 8

Scrub the potatoes and poke with the tines of a fork. Wrap with aluminum foil and place around hot coals in the grill. Cook for 30 to 45 minutes, and rotate the potatoes halfway through the cooking. Potatoes will be ready when they feel tender when squeezed with an oven mitt.

Remove from the foil and cut potatoes in half lengthwise and scoop out meat, Select 6 to 8 of the nicest shells, leaving a thin shell of meat around the edges. Reserve the meat for stuffing and discard the excess shells.

Mash the reserved meat in a large mixing bowl. Add the cream, sour cream, margarine, garlic puree, salt, and pepper, stirring until the mixture is mostly smooth. Let cool.

Spoon the mixture into a large resealable plastic bag. Snip off a corner of the bag and pipe the mixture into the reserved shells, filling to above edges of the shells. Place the potatoes in a foil pan in a single layer and top with the cheddar cheese and decoratively garnish with the Budha's All-Purpose Rub. Potatoes can be covered with foil and refrigerated or frozen. Before serving, place in a 350-degree smoker or oven and bake for 25 to 30 minutes.

Pumpkin Tiramisu

¼ cup hot brewed espresso

¼ cup brandy

1 package ladyfingers

8 ounces cream cheese, at
    room temperature

15-ounce can pumpkin puree

1 teaspoon ground cinnamon

1 teaspoon ground ginger

½ teaspoon ground nutmeg

1 teaspoon unsweetened
    cocoa powder

1½ cups powdered sugar

1 teaspoon vanilla extract

2½ cups heavy or whipping
    cream, whipped and
    chilled

Serves 10

In a shallow bowl, combine the espresso and brandy. Dip the ladyfingers in the mixture and use half of them to line the bottom of a 9x9-inch pan.

Mix the cream cheese with the pumpkin, spices, cocoa powder, powdered sugar, and vanilla, whipping until smooth. Fold in 1½ cups of the whipped cream. Spread half of the mixture over the ladyfingers. Add a second layer of ladyfingers dipped in espresso mixture and cover with the remaining pumpkin mixture. Gently spread the remaining whipped cream on top of the mixture. Sprinkle decoratively with additional cinnamon and cocoa. Cover and chill for at least 2 hours or overnight.

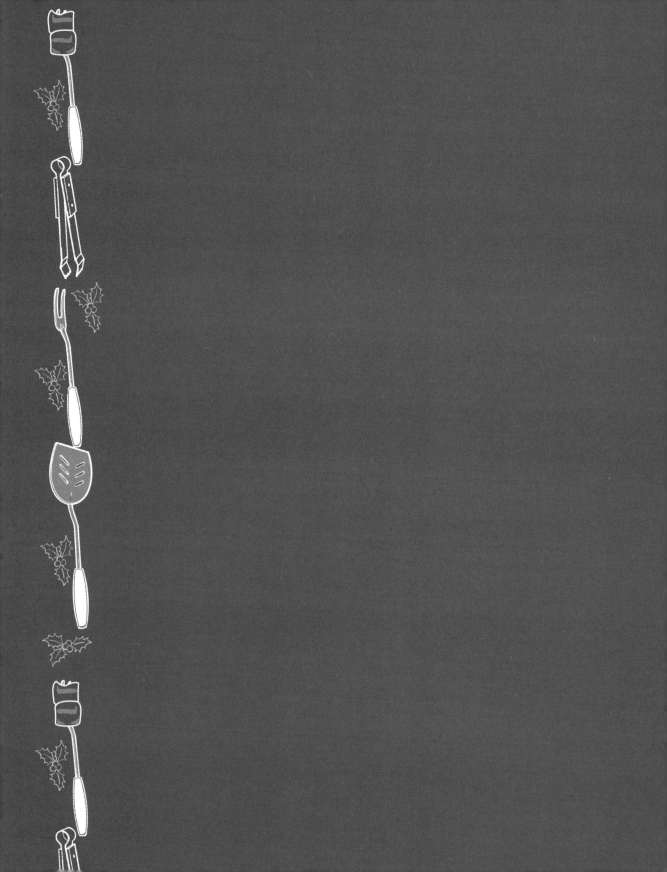

Chapter 3

Christmas Eve

I was an orphan as a kid. I had parents and a home—but I say that because I would lend myself to whichever family had the most action going on Christmas Eve. There were always families that opened up their Christmas gifts on Christmas Eve, and if I came over often enough or for many years in a row, they'd get something for me. And on Christmas Eve there was always lots of candy, tons of nuts, and hot beverages that kids could enjoy, of course without the liqueur enhancements that the older folks enjoyed.

Now us grown-ups can pour the booze freely, if we so desire, and make the most of some of those delicious toddy and eggnog drinks. And if you're so inclined, you can really amaze your holiday friends—and their drop-by guests—with an incredible celebratory dinner to ring in the cheer.

Christmas Eve is the last day of Advent, and as such fish is the perfect dish. You can have clams, oysters, and seafood of all kinds. We've had 25 to 30 people in our house, serving dishes like creamed oysters, grilled shrimp, and a garnish of ham to make it tasty. Here are some of our favorite Christmas Eve recipes to get into the spirit of the season.

Whole Roast Striped Bass with Herb Stuffing

5-pound striped bass, scaled
    and gutted

Stuffing:

1 cup Italian flat-leaf parsley

2 shallots, minced

4 tablespoons olive oil

1 cup fine bread crumbs

Juice and zest of 1 lemon

Striped bass is one of the finest fish in the sea. And, when it comes from cold, Atlantic waters, its wonderful, firm white flesh is moist and juicy. When you do this recipe, you can leave the head on, but only if that won't offend your guests!

Serves 8 to 10 (depending on what else you are serving)

Mix all the stuffing ingredients together. Spread it evenly in the fish. Tie the fish securely with kitchen string that you have pre-soaked so that it will not burn.

Set your grill at 300 degrees, or make a bed of coals that are slowed down to about 300 degrees. Make sure the grid is 6 to 8 inches from the flame.

Place the fish on a piece of aluminum foil and grill 12 minutes per side to brown. Close lid of the grill and turn the heat down and grill another 8 to 10 minutes, until the fish is piping hot.

BIG DADDY LOWDOWN

Grilled Chicken of the Sea

The nonfatty fish, such as swordfish, shark, and tuna, usually grill up the best.

Skewered BBQ Shrimp with Coconut Rice

24 jumbo shrimp, 2 per
skewer, shelled and
cleaned
12 wooden skewers, soaked
in water for at least 1
hour

Sauce:
1 cup bottled chili sauce
Juice of 1 lime
2 cloves garlic, minced
1 tablespoon Worcestershire
sauce
1 teaspoon red pepper flakes
(or to taste)
2 tablespoons unsalted
butter

This is as simple as it is excellent, and can be either an hors d'oeuvre or a main course.

Serves 6 as an entrée

Mix the sauce ingredients in a small pot and warm until the butter melts.

Set your grill on high or make a bed of hot coals.

Dip the shrimp in the sauce. String them on the prepared skewers.

Grill the shrimp about 45 seconds per side. Serve with coconut rice.

Rice: Follow the directions on the box of any good rice, but substitute 1 cup coconut milk for 1 cup of water required and garnish with chopped macadamia nuts.

Planked Wild Salmon with Dill Sauce

Sauce:

1 cup good mayonnaise

½ cup olive oil

2 egg yolks

½ cup minced red onion

1 teaspoon dried dill weed

1 clove garlic

Juice and zest of 1 lemon

Fish:

16x8-inch cedar plank

3-pound wild salmon fillet

½ stick butter

Juice of ½ lemon

2 tablespoons Dijon-style
   mustard

1 teaspoon dried dill weed

Salt and pepper to taste

Use a nice piece of cedar, which you have sanded. Make the sauce in advance and serve it on the side.

Serves 8 to 10

Whirl all the sauce ingredients in the jar of your blender. Place in a bowl, cover, and refrigerate.

Soak the plank for 3 hours.

Heat the grill to medium-high.

Melt the butter and add the lemon juice, mustard, and dill weed.

BIG DADDY LOWDOWN

Best Catch of the Day?

A bright, skinny fillet. Fresh fish should never smell "fishy"—and if it does, it has already begun to go bad. It should never have a dull, opaque look to it.

Rinse the fish in cold water, pat dry with paper towels, and sprinkle it with salt and pepper.

Place the plank on the grill and let it toast for 4 to 5 minutes. When it smokes, turn the plank and put the fish on it. Paint the fish with the melted butter mixture.

Place the plank back on the grill and roast it for 15 to 20 minutes, or until the fish flakes.

Place the plank on a platter and serve with the sauce on the side.

Oysters on the Half Shell with Casino Butter Topping

24 large sweet oysters, freshly opened

A large baking pan filled with rock salt

Casino butter:

1 stick unsalted butter, at room temperature

4 slices of bacon, par-cooked, not crisp, cut in small pieces

2 cloves garlic, minced

Freshly ground black pepper to taste

½ cup dry bread crumbs

3 tablespoons grated Parmesan

Lemon wedges and toasted bread

This is a fantastic appetizer. Have your fishmonger open the oysters, and make sure that he doesn't rinse the juices off them. Serve hot with cubes of toasted bread to sop up the juices in the shells!

Serves 6

Set your broiler at 400 degrees, or your grill on medium-high.

Place the opened oysters on the pan, pressing them into the rock salt so they won't tip. Using a fork, mix the butter, bacon, garlic, pepper, and bread crumbs. Spoon on top of the oysters, dividing evenly. Sprinkle with the Parmesan cheese.

Broil 8 inches from flame until bacon sizzles and butter melts; don't overcook. They shouldn't take more than 5 minutes to cook on high heat. Overcooked oysters are tough. Serve with lemon wedges and pieces of toasted bread.

Grilled Clams
with Garlic Sauce over Pasta

1 pound linguini or angel-
hair pasta

24 littleneck clams (small
quahogs), well scrubbed

Sauce:

¼ cup olive oil

½ stick unsalted butter

¼ cup finely chopped fennel
bulb

4 cloves chopped garlic, or
to taste

1 cup bottled clam broth

½ cup dry white wine

½ cup chopped Italian flat-
leaf parsley

1 teaspoon red pepper
flakes, or to taste

This is great! The clams get a smoky taste from the grill, especially if you use wood chips on the fire.

Serves 4

Make the sauce in advance. Heat the olive oil and butter. Sauté the fennel and garlic until softened but not browned. Mix in the rest of the ingredients, bring to a boil, and set aside.

Put the pasta in a large pot of boiling hot water.

Grill the clams over hot fire until they just begin to open. Add them to the sauce.

Carefully put the pasta into the pan of sauce. Mix gently and serve in warm bowls.

Note: Although some people put cheese on clam sauce, we do not!

BIG DADDY LOWDOWN

A Tip for Preparing Seafood on the Grill

Oil the seafood before placing it on the grill to prevent it from sticking and breaking up.

Grilled Diver Scallops
with North Carolina–Style Mustard Sauce

20 to 30 diver scallops,
     depending on size, rinsed

Sauce:
3 egg yolks

1 clove garlic

1 tablespoon white wine
     vinegar

1 tablespoon Dijon-style
     mustard

¾ cup olive oil

Diver scallops are huge, weighing about 3 ounces each. One or two is enough for a serving, and one is plenty for an hors d'oeuvre. Because scallops are delicate, do not overpower them with sauce or spices. There's no sense in buying a very expensive seafood, especially if you can't taste it!

Serves 10 as an hors d'oeuvre

Place the egg yolks, garlic, vinegar, and mustard in the jar of your blender. Whirl until well blended.

Very slowly add the oil, giving the eggs time to "digest" the oil. The sauce should have the consistency of mayonnaise.

Set your grill on high.

Place the scallops on skewers and brush lightly with the sauce.

Grill 1 minute per side—if you overcook them they will get tough!

Grilled Squid with Spanish Sauce

18 baby squid (about 3-inch-
long tubes, tentacles on
the side)
½ cup olive oil

Sauce:
1 cup heavy or whipping
cream
2 bags baby spinach,
chopped
Salt and pepper to taste
Juice of 1 lemon

This is sooo Mediterranean with a touch of American ingenuity! Baby squid require very little cooking; they are done as soon as they are really hot. We love the tentacles, but don't use them if they bother you. This is a great buffet dish, beautifully arranged on a warm platter.

Serves 6 to 8

Place the cream in a large saucepan and boil until it's reduced by half.

Add the spinach, salt, and pepper and reduce heat to warm.

After removing from stove, add lemon juice.

Brush each squid tube with the olive oil. Place on a grid about the size of chicken wire.

Place on a very hot fire or coals and grill 1 minute per side.

Arrange on a platter with sauce in a bowl in the center and lemon wedges placed around the squid.

Baked Brie with Sun-Dried Tomatoes

2 ounces sun-dried
   tomatoes, drained
Salt and freshly ground
   black pepper to taste
5-inch round of Brie
1 sheet frozen puff pastry,
   defrosted

This is creamy and delicious! The Brie gets runny and the puff pastry crisps up!

Serves 6 to 8

Chop the tomatoes and add salt and pepper.

Unwrap the Brie and place it on the sheet of pastry. Spread the Brie with sun-dried tomato pieces, burying the pieces in the pastry as you go. Fold the pastry up around the Brie.

Bake for 20 minutes in a 325-degree oven.

Seafood Salad Misto

1 pound large shrimp,
  shelled and cleaned
1 pound squid, cleaned and
  cut into tubes
1 pound clams, scrubbed
1 pound mussels, scrubbed
Bed of mixed greens,
  washed and set aside
½ lemon, cut in small pieces

Dressing:

1 cup olive oil
¼ cup champagne vinegar
Pinch sugar
Salt and pepper to taste
½ teaspoon Worcestershire
  sauce
½ cup fresh parsley, rinsed
  and minced

This is another perfect dish for a buffet. It's refreshing and not too filling. You can cook the seafood the day before and refrigerate it. You can also make the dressing the day before. Assemble the salad when your guests arrive. Leave the shells on the clams and mussels; just be sure they are well scrubbed before you cook them.

Serves 10 to 12

Boil the shrimp and squid for 3 minutes in the same pot. Drain and place in a bowl.

Place the clams and mussels in a pot and steam them open. Save the juice for soup and drain the seafood, adding it to the bowl of shrimp and squid. When cool, cover and refrigerate.

Mix the dressing ingredients and refrigerate it until just before serving.

Gently mix the seafood with the dressing. Arrange on a bed of greens and garnish with lemon.

Wild Rice Casserole

1½ cups wild rice

8 cups water

1 teaspoon salt

¾ stick butter

6 ounces exotic mushrooms,
such as criminis or
shiitakes, cleaned and
chopped

1 teaspoon dried thyme
leaves, or 3 teaspoons
fresh thyme

¼ cup heavy or whipping
cream

½ cup fresh bread crumbs

This is great with salmon or bass. Don't pay one bit of attention to the directions on the box or package of wild rice—it takes 2 hours to cook no matter what they say! You can make this a day ahead and refrigerate it; just warm it before serving.

Serves 10

Rinse the rice. Bring a pot of salted water to a boil. Add the rice and return to a boil. Turn the heat to a simmer and cover. Check every 15 minutes, stirring to prevent clumping. The rice is done when it's "bloomed," no more little spiky grains but little flowers! Let the rice cool.

Melt the butter in a saucepan. Add the mushrooms and sauté gently until softened.

Add the thyme and cream.

Butter or use nonstick spray in a 3-quart casserole. Mix the rice and mushrooms in the casserole and dot with butter. Sprinkle with the bread crumbs and heat.

Baby Artichoke Salad
with Gorgonzola and Walnuts

Dressing:

1 tablespoon lemon juice

1 tablespoon red wine
vinegar

1 teaspoon prepared mustard

2 cloves garlic

2 shallots

1 tablespoon fresh or dried
rosemary leaves

1 teaspoon hot red pepper
sauce

Salt to taste

Salad:

2 boxes frozen artichoke
hearts

Mixed greens (baby spinach,
Bibb or Boston lettuce,
and a little iceberg)

2 ounces Gorgonzola
cheese, crumbled

½ cup walnuts, toasted

The frozen artichoke hearts are perfect for this dish. And they save you an immense amount of time!

Serves 6 to 8

Whirl all the dressing ingredients in the jar of your blender and store in the refrigerator.

Cut the artichokes in half and boil about 10 minutes, until tender. Cool.

Place the artichokes on a platter lined with the greens and sprinkle with the dressing, cheese, and walnuts.

Rustic Flan with Raspberries

1 cup heavy or whipping
  cream
1 box (about 1 pound) sliced
  frozen peaches or canned
  peaches, drained
8 ounces fresh raspberries,
  washed, dried on a paper
  towel, and set aside
¼ cup Chambord or other
  raspberry liqueur

Flan:
1¼ cups milk
2 teaspoons white or light
  brown sugar
4 eggs
1 teaspoon pure vanilla
  extract
Pinch salt
1 cup all-purpose flour
1 tablespoon baking powder

Flan is custard. This one is rustic, a country dessert. It's easy but festive because of the peaches, raspberry liqueur, and fresh raspberries. In the old days, people canned their peaches, or froze them. They did not use liqueurs or packaged frozen peaches.

Serves 6 to 8

Whip the cream and set aside.

Mix the sliced peaches, raspberries, and raspberry liqueur in a bowl and set aside.

Set your oven at 350 degrees. Spray a glass pie plate with nonstick spray.

Mix all the flan ingredients in the jar of your blender. Whirl until well blended and doubled in volume.

Pour a thin skim (⅛ inch) of the batter into the bottom of the prepared pie plate.

Bake the batter in the oven for 5 minutes. Add the marinated fruits.

Cover with the rest of the batter. Bake for 50 to 60 minutes.

To assemble: When the flan is puffed and set, let cool until just warm.

Spread with the whipped cream, cut into wedges, and serve warm.

Grilled Pineapple
with Nuts and Berry Coulis

Coulis:

1 cup raspberries

1 cup strawberries

¼ cup rum

¼ cup white sugar

Pineapple:

1 cup macadamia nuts

½ stick butter, melted

¼ cup packed brown sugar

8 rounds of fresh pineapple,
    cored and cut in ½-inch
    slices

This is colorful, delicious, and easy to make! Get the grill going for other parts of the dinner and just after you've eaten, pop the pineapple on the grill. Have everything else ready and assemble at the last minute.

Serves 8

Mix all the coulis ingredients in the blender and set aside.

Toast the nuts until lightly browned, then chop. Set aside.

Mix together the butter and brown sugar. Lay the pineapple slices on a baking sheet and spread with the butter mixture.

Grill until the sugar caramelizes. Drizzle with the coulis and sprinkle with the nuts. Serve warm.

Chapter 4

Christmas Day

You may want to sleep late, but there are kids in the place that will be up at the crack of dawn. Then there are the friends and relatives who are going to be dropping in at noon, and they're going to be hungry. So even if you were playing Santa the night before, you're going to have to be up and at 'em come Christmas morning. Grilling is the perfect way to handle the well-wishers and holiday revelers. Have your friends sing carols as you prepare special holiday roasts, leaving them on low temperatures for long periods of time, enabling you time to enjoy the spirit of the moment.

If you're really lucky, your loved ones will honor you with gifts and presents that will enhance your grilling experience. Make sure to prepare a wish list that has such items as a rib rack, cedar grilling planks, or grill basket.

White Christmas warning to those of you in the Northeast: Always keep a clear path from the house to the grill. You don't want to slip and fall and spend your holiday in the nearest hospital emergency room.

Grill-Roasted Goose with Side of Dried-Fruit Stuffing

10 cups of any of the stuffing recipes listed in this book

Rub of herbs and spices:

1 teaspoon *each* of salt, pepper, lemon zest, orange zest, onion powder, minced fresh ginger, rosemary leaves, and dried thyme leaves, and ½ teaspoon ground cloves

Stock made with goose wings, innards, and chicken broth

10- to 12-pound goose, rinsed and patted dry, innards removed for stock

2 quarts simmering water for basting

2 cups chicken broth

The great thing about goose is its exceptional flavor, unlike other poultry. And, once you've prepared it properly, you'll have it time and again for fall and winter feasting, no matter what the occasion. Serve it with any good fruity stuffing, both in the goose and on the side.

Serves 12 to 16

Prepare the stuffing in advance and refrigerate. Do not stuff the goose until the last minute.

In a small bowl, mix the rub ingredients together and set aside.

Snip the wings off the goose and place in a stockpot with innards, 2 cups chicken broth, and a teaspoon of the rub. Simmer for gravy.

Set the fire or gas at 400 degrees. Rub the goose inside and out with the rub mixture. Stuff the goose and tie the legs closed.

Bring the 2 quarts water to a simmer.

Place the stuffed goose in an aluminum-foil roasting pan over the coals or gas flame. Add some wood chips to the fire for extra flavor.

Sear the goose quickly, then either reduce heat to 350 degrees or go to indirect heating.

Prick the goose with a fork; do not pierce the

meat, only the fat. Baste with the simmering water every 15 minutes. Prick the skin 2 or 3 more times.

Using a bulb baster, remove the excess water and fat from the roasting pan.

This should take 2½ hours if the heat is consistent, and the goose should come to 150 degrees internally. Bake the extra stuffing for 30 minutes before serving, basting with a bit of the stock.

Place the goose on a warm platter to rest for 15 minutes before carving. Make the gravy by adding 2 tablespoons flour to the brown bits in the pan. Cook in a medium saucepan, stirring until very smooth. Add the hot stock. Serve on the side. We enjoy this with Pureed Chestnuts (see page 74).

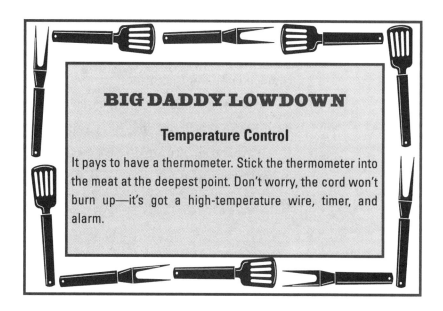

BIG DADDY LOWDOWN

Temperature Control

It pays to have a thermometer. Stick the thermometer into the meat at the deepest point. Don't worry, the cord won't burn up—it's got a high-temperature wire, timer, and alarm.

Pureed Chestnuts

1 pound fresh chestnuts, or
    1 cup from a jar or can,
    unsweetened
1 tablespoon butter
¼ cup cream (more if
    chestnuts are fresh and
    dry roasted)
½ teaspoon salt and pepper
    to taste (chestnuts are
    naturally sweet; you may
    want to add more salt)

You can roast or boil chestnuts and then shell and skin them. We find chestnuts that are shelled, cooked, and either canned or in a jar are the easiest to use and ready instantly.

Makes 1¼ cups

Prepare the chestnuts if fresh. Cut X's in the shells with a sharp knife. Roast at 400 degrees until they split open. When cool enough to handle, remove shells and skins.

Drain the jar or can. In a saucepan, heat chestnuts and butter over low heat until butter melts. Place warm chestnuts in the food processor and pulse until fine. Add cream, salt, and pepper. Pulse until pureed. If dry, add a bit more cream.

Standing Prime Ribs of Beef

8-pound best cut standing
    rib roast, prime if you can
    get it

2 minced shallots

Salt and pepper to taste

Basting sauce of 2 cups beef
    broth, 1 cup dry red wine,
    2 bay leaves, and 1
    teaspoon dried thyme
    leaves

Onions, carrots, celery, and
    potatoes to surround the
    roast

This is a traditional Olde English Christmas dinner. And, when you serve it with puffy and delicious Yorkshire pudding, it's especially wonderful!

Serves 10 to 12

Leave the meat out for 1 hour before roasting. Trim off excess fat and place in a pot to render for the Yorkshire pudding.

Add minced shallot and 1 cup water to the beef fat, cover, and simmer until melted.

BIG DADDY LOWDOWN

Prime Tips for Prime Rib

Take the prime rib and put a wet marinade on about an hour before cooking. Once you're ready to go, cook it whole, and take a peek after about three hours to check on degree of doneness, then keep the lid closed. You can use the drippings from the pan to make a sauce by adding white wine, Worcestershire sauce, or soy sauce. For a Christmas Day dinner, you might start at about 10 a.m., and serve the prime rib in the late afternoon.

Set your grill at 400 degrees.

Rub the meat with salt and pepper and place in a pan. Sear and then baste every 15 minutes. Add the vegetables and potatoes. Roast for 1 hour for rare, 90 minutes for medium, and 1¾ hours for medium-well. Let the beef rest for 30 minutes before carving.

Bake Yorkshire Pudding (see page 90) while beef is resting.

Make gravy by adding flour to the roasting pan, whisk, and then add the rest of the basting liquid.

Pepper-Crusted Sirloin Steak

5- to 6-pound sirloin, 2
    inches thick, bone-in
1 tablespoon Worcestershire
    sauce
1 teaspoon *each* black, red,
    and white peppercorns,
    crushed
½ teaspoon cayenne pepper
Coarse sea salt or kosher
    salt to taste

We love this on the grill with a few good soaked hickory chips to impart a smoky flavor. The more kinds of pepper you can use, the better!

Serves 8 to 10

Place the steak on a work surface and let come to room temperature an hour before cooking.

Set the grill at 375 degrees.

Rub the steak with the Worcestershire sauce and then mix the crushed peppercorns and cayenne with salt. Rub the pepper mixture into the steak, pressing into the flesh.

Place the steak on a 450-degree grill and sear on both sides. Turn the heat down and grill until it's the right level of doneness. Let the meat rest for 10 minutes before carving.

BIG DADDY LOWDOWN

Tips for Grilling Steaks from Morton's of Chicago

- Bring 'em in from out of the cold. Steaks should be at room temperature before grilling.
- Check the oil. Before you begin, lightly oil the grilling rack. It keeps the meat from sticking and tearing—and losing its natural juices.
- It's got to be hot! Preheat the grill to 600 to 800 degrees and keep it at that temperature for 30 to 45 minutes before putting the steaks on. It's during the first few minutes of grilling that the high temperature sears the meat, forming the coating that seals in those tasty juices. High direct heat is almost as important as the meat itself.
- Use a seasoned approach: Add a bit of seasoning before placing the steak on the grill. Some salt and pepper can do wonders.

Herb-and-Garlic-Crusted Baby Racks of Lamb

3 racks of lamb, 1½ pounds
    each (remember, the
    bones weigh a lot)
Salt and pepper to taste

Crust:

3 cloves garlic, crushed and
    minced
3 tablespoons chopped fresh
    rosemary
3 tablespoons chopped
    parsley
Juice of ½ lemon
½ cup olive oil

A young, juicy baby rack of lamb is one of the real treats, though expensive. It's also very quick and easy to prepare and elegant to serve. But please, skip the mint jelly! It's an insult to this delicate meat.

Serves 6 to 9

Trim the lamb; the fat is strong. Sprinkle with salt and pepper.

Set your grill at 500 degrees. Let the lamb come to room temperature before roasting.

Mix the ingredients for the crust and set aside.

Grill the lamb meat side down, then bone side down 5 minutes per side. Place in a roasting pan bone side down. Press the crust ingredients into the meat. Return to the grill and roast for another 8 to 10 minutes for a nice pink rack. Remove lamb, and let rest for 5 minutes. Cut into chops and serve. This is best when pink on the inside and crusty on the outside.

Saddle (Rack or Rib Roast) of Venison

4 pounds rack of venison,
    rinsed, patted dry, and
    placed on a roasting pan
    to come to room
    temperature
Coarse salt

Rub:

1 tablespoon juniper berries,
    crushed
1 tablespoon black
    peppercorns, crushed
1 tablespoon dried rosemary
    leaves, crumbled
½ stick unsalted butter, at
    room temperature

Basting sauce:

1 cup beef broth (canned
    is fine)
1 cup red vermouth

Venison is not "gamey" in flavor. Ideally, it's sweet and tender with almost no fat! Because of its leanness you need to add bacon or some basting sauce with a bit of butter in it. Hunters and gourmets alike insist that venison be served rare unless you are making a stew. And, if you are stewing, you'd never use a saddle or rack of venison.

Serves 6 to 8

Set your grill at 400 degrees. Sprinkle the meat with salt. Mix the rub ingredients together and spread over the meat, rubbing in well.

Roast the meat on indirect heat in an aluminum-foil pan for 35 minutes, basting every 10 minutes. It's done when the internal temperature comes to 120 degrees. It will continue to cook with internal thermal heating. Cover with aluminum foil and let rest for 20 minutes.

Make a simple sauce with the basting liquid and any juices remaining in the pan.

Grill-Roasted Sirloin Roast of Bison (or Buffalo)

5- to 6-pound sirloin of bison, patted dry

Marinade and basting sauce:

1 cup dry red wine

½ cup olive oil

1 teaspoon juniper berries, crushed

1 clove garlic, minced

½ cup olive or vegetable oil

Salt and pepper to taste

Gravy:

2 teaspoons all-purpose flour

Pan drippings

1 cup beef broth

Salt and pepper to taste

The American bison was once slaughtered almost to extinction. These huge animals sustained Native Americans for many centuries, plus the U.S. Cavalry and the early settlers of the plains, until they got in the way of cattle herds. And so, Americans fell in love with beef. Fortunately, a few ranchers have preserved the bison (or buffalo) and we are beginning to get a taste of our American heritage! Bison is much leaner than beef, and it's grass-fed for a lighter taste and less fat. It's also readily available on the Web if you can't find it at your local grocery store.

Serves 8 to 10

Place the bison roast in a plastic bag with the marinade ingredients. Seal and move around to make sure the meat is coated. Marinate for 8 to 12 hours in the refrigerator.

Set your grill at 500 degrees. Remove the meat, reserving the marinade. Place the meat in a shallow roasting pan.

Sear the meat, then reduce the flame to 275 degrees.

Baste with the marinade. The roast is done

when a meat thermometer deeply inserted reaches 135 degrees. Let the roast rest for 20 minutes, loosely covered with aluminum foil.

To make the gravy, stir the flour into the drippings and blend, cooking at a simmer on top of the stove.

Add the broth and stir. Add salt and pepper. Bring to a boil and serve in a gravy boat. Serve the roast with roasted vegetables.

BIG DADDY LOWDOWN

Liquid Measure

For marinades or rubs based on mild liquids, you'll need about 1 cup for every 2 to 3 pounds.

Grill-Roast Turkey—Orange Flavored

Half of a 10-pound turkey, split

1 teaspoon coarse salt

1 orange, juice squeezed out, skin and pith finely chopped

1 teaspoon dried thyme leaves, or 1 tablespoon fresh lemon thyme

2 tablespoons butter, at room temperature

Freshly ground black pepper to taste

1 tablespoon olive oil

This recipe is good and festive at any time of year. Have your butcher split a young, small turkey from neck to tail. Either do both for a crowd or freeze half for future cooking.

Rinse the turkey, pat dry on paper towels, and generously salt the turkey inside and out.

Reserve the squeezed orange juice for future use.

Mix the chopped orange, thyme, and butter. Add pepper to taste.

Tease the orange butter under the skin of the turkey, gently pushing it down to the thigh and leg.

Set your grill at 400 degrees. Place the turkey in an aluminum roasting pan.

Rub the olive oil into the skin. Roast the turkey at 400 degrees for 10 minutes, then reduce the heat to 300 degrees and close the grill lid. Roast until the internal temperature reaches 145 degrees.

Let the turkey rest for 15 minutes before carving. Serve with cranberry relish and turkey gravy.

Smitty's Award-Winning Bar-B-Que Pork Tenderloin

4 tablespoons paprika

¼ cup packed brown sugar

2 tablespoons white sugar

2 tablespoons kosher salt

1 teaspoon ground cumin

1 teaspoon black pepper

1 teaspoon cayenne pepper

Two 2-pound pork
   tenderloins

⅓ cup Dijon-style mustard

1 pound thick-cut bacon

Apple-mango juice, in spray
   bottle

2 cups barbecue sauce,
   optional

We met Brian Smith and his team, Smitty's Bar-B-Que, at the Lenexa Barbecue Battle, and used this award-winning tenderloin recipe in our first book. We're coming back to it again now, first because it's *that* good and makes for the perfect Christmas table dish, sliced up on a silver serving platter. Second, because we've got Smitty's team prepping the dish on the attached DVD, and once you've watched them make it you'll waste no time following along to try it yourself. It's sweet, spicy, and the bacon may be the best stocking stuffer you'll see this season, whether you were naughty or nice!

Serves 6 to 10

Mix the paprika through the cayenne pepper in a small bowl. Coat the mixture evenly over the pork tenderloins, place in a resealable food storage bag, and let marinate in the refrigerator overnight.

Empty one bag of hickory chunks into a bucket filled with water, and let soak overnight.

Remove the tenderloin from the bag, and coat with the Dijon mustard. Wrap each piece in bacon from end to end.

Ignite the charcoal in a chimney starter. Brian suggests letting it burn for the amount of time it takes the average guy to drink a 12-ounce cold beverage before placing several chunks of the wet hickory onto the coals. Maintain a temperature of about 220 degrees.

Place the meat on the rack. Cook at 2 hours per pound, about 4 hours total.

After about 3 hours, spray the meat with apple-mango juice.

Remove the meat from the grill, and unwrap bacon. If using barbecue sauce, heat in a small saucepan before serving. Slice the meat, and enjoy. The bacon can be eaten on the spot, or crumbled up and used to make a batch of smoky baked beans.

Mincemeat Pie with Pork, Beef, and Dried Fruit

Filling:

1 cup dark rum

½ cup white raisins

1 cup pitted prunes, chopped

¼ cup vegetable oil

½ cup shallots, chopped

8 ounces ground beef

8 ounces ground pork

Salt and freshly ground
    black pepper to taste

1 teaspoon orange or lemon
    zest

½ teaspoon ground cloves

½ teaspoon ground cinnamon

½ teaspoon ground nutmeg

1 teaspoon brown sugar

2 tablespoons Wondra
    quick-blending flour

Crust:

Dough for a 2-crust pie, your
    own, refrigerated, or
    frozen

This is a classic from the past that is still a great part of modern tradition! Small pieces make a really good buffet offering.

Serves 8 to 10

Set your grill at 400 degrees on indirect heat (or use your oven).

Warm the rum and soak the dried fruit in it for 1 hour.

Sauté the shallots in the oil. Add the meat and brown lightly.

Stir in the dried fruits and the rest of the ingredients, mixing well.

Spray a 9- or 10-inch pie pan with nonstick spray. Line the bottom with the crust.

Heap in the filling mixture. Cover with the top crust and bake at 400 degrees for 15 minutes, reduce the heat to 325 degrees, and bake for 45 minutes.

Grilled Figs with Mascarpone and Gorgonzola Whip over Baby Spinach

2 bags baby spinach

½ cup any good balsamic vinaigrette

½ cup mascarpone cheese

¼ cup Gorgonzola cheese, crumbled

12 fresh Mission figs, split in half

This is a delicious salad with creative ingredients.

Serves 6

Place the spinach greens on plates or arrange them on a platter.

Drizzle the greens with the vinaigrette. Whip together the mascarpone and Gorgonzola cheeses.

Grill the figs for 2 to 3 minutes per side and arrange on the spinach, cut side up.

Drop a bit of the cheese whip on top of each fig and serve.

Shrimp Bisque

2 pounds shrimp, peeled and
    cleaned, shells reserved

½ cup dry white wine

2 cups water

¼ cup parsley

1 teaspoon tomato paste

½ stick unsalted butter

2 shallots, chopped

2 large carrots, chopped

Salt and freshly ground
    black pepper to taste

2 tablespoons Wondra
    quick-blending flour

¼ cup sherry

2 cups heavy or whipping
    cream

¼ teaspoon cayenne pepper

This is a festive soup that can be served hot in the winter and chilled in the summer.

Makes 6 cups

Place the shrimp shells in a pan in the oven and toast—be careful not to burn.

Put the shells, wine, and water in a large saucepan and simmer for 20 minutes.

Blend the shells in a food processor and strain the liquid into the saucepan. Stir in the parsley, tomato paste, and shrimp.

Cook for 2 to 3 minutes, stirring until the shrimp turns pink. Melt the butter and sauté the shallots and carrots for 8 minutes.

Add salt and pepper. Add flour to thicken.

Whirl in the jar of your blender and return to the saucepan. Stir in the sherry, then the cream. Heat but do not boil, and serve.

Grilled Butternut Squash with Buttery Pecans

Pecans:

2 tablespoons butter

1 cup pecans

Salt and pepper to taste

Pinch ground nutmeg

Squash:

3 acorn squash, split, seeds
   scraped out

2 tablespoons butter

This delicious winter dish is great with a little honey or maple syrup.

Serves 6

Using a sauté pan, melt the butter and add the pecans and spices. Set aside.

Set the grill at 350 degrees. Line with a sheet of aluminum foil. Place the squash cut side down on the foil. Roast for 25 minutes, or until a knife tip pierces the squash easily. Turn the squash, add the butter, and continue to roast for another 10 minutes.

Place on a warm platter and spoon the pecans into the squash cups.

Yorkshire Pudding

2 cups all-purpose flour,
  sifted

1 cup light cream

1 cup whole milk

4 eggs

Salt and pepper to taste

8 tablespoons beef fat,
  bacon drippings, butter, or
  lard

Yorkshire pudding will be served with the beef or lamb. This is basically a puffy custard based in some good fat. It must be made in advance, baked at the last minute. It's meant to soak up the drippings from the meat and is very delicious. You can render fat, as in the Standing Prime Ribs of Beef recipe. And if you have super-lean meat, simply use butter, lard, or oil.

Serves 8 to 12

Sift the flour into a bowl. Beat in the cream and milk. Add eggs one at a time. Mix in salt and pepper to taste.

Cover the batter and refrigerate for 2 to 3 hours. Take out of the fridge 1 hour before serving.

Spoon beef fat into a metal pan, about 1 inch deep, or if you are cooking venison or bison, use bacon drippings, butter, or lard.

Place the pan in a 450-degree oven until fat sizzles. Give the batter a quick whisk and pour into the hot pan. Bake for 15 minutes, then reduce the heat to 350 degrees and bake for another 10 to 15 minutes. The pudding should be light and crispy on the outside and moist on the inside.

Cut into squares and serve on a warm platter or around the roast.

Grilled d'Anjou Pears

6 firm, ripe pears, peeled,
    cored, and cut in half
1 teaspoon butter
1 teaspoon lemon juice
½ teaspoon dried rosemary
    or thyme leaves,
    crumbled
Salt and pepper to taste

This makes a luscious side dish and only takes a few minutes.

Serves 6 to 8

Place the pears on a very hot grill for 30 seconds per side. Place in a small saucepan and add the butter, lemon juice, rosemary or thyme, salt and pepper. Mash gently and serve warm.

Chocolate Espresso Mousse

1 envelope unflavored
   gelatin
¼ cup cool water
2 squares bittersweet
   chocolate
1 cup brewed strong, instant
   espresso
2 tablespoons Kahlua or
   other chocolate liqueur
1 tablespoon dark rum
½ teaspoon salt, or to taste
4 egg whites
1 cup heavy or whipping
   cream
1 pint fresh red raspberries

This is very festive, and made more so with the addition of a few fresh raspberries for garnish.

Serves 6 to 8

Place the gelatin and water in your blender. Melt the chocolate in the espresso coffee. Add the Kahlua and dark rum. Whirl in the blender until smooth and place in a large bowl. Let cool to room temperature.

Whip the egg whites until stiff and fold into the chocolate mixture.

Whip the cream and fold into the chocolate mixture.

Chill for 2 hours, minimum, stirring gently from bottom to top to ensure that the gelatin mixture does not settle on the bottom.

Serve in wineglasses and garnish with fresh raspberries.

Chapter 5

New Year's Day: Celebratory Buffet

When we were kids, my best friend's parents held this fancy New Year's Day party. These were always elegant and in some ways more important to them than New Year's Eve. We made the rounds serving champagne and got our first look at hungover and newly inebriated party guests.

New Year's Day is a sophisticated holiday, and dishes are a little leaner because you've been eating all week long. Yet it is the last gasp of the holiday—so you want it to be really delicious! We used to have a filet mignon ready to cook per each person's taste in a bubbling Burgundy sauce as people came and went all afternoon. People would say they couldn't eat another bite—hungover or whatever—but they always ended up eating and eating.

Now that we're big boys and girls we can be the ones to have all the fun. We advocate a wholesome bottle of champagne, be it Taitinger or Dom

Perignon, and lots of goodies to go with it. Bloody Marys or Virgin Marys are also appropriate, as is Irish coffee. We've picked some delicate and delicious party favorites reminiscent of the kinds of good times we used to have, along with some chic new tips. Our favorite appetizer is the Deviled Pullet Eggs with Caviar. It's sure to make members of the opposite sex just fall in love with you.

By the way, if you have one too many champagnes, you should have a "designated griller" to help you out, if not one or two of your friends. Better yet, find some ambitious kids looking to help out and see how the adults live it up on the day after.

Pepper-Roast Almonds and Champagne

1 tablespoon *each* freshly
    ground black, white, and
    pink pepper

2 teaspoons salt

½ stick unsalted butter

¾ cup packed light brown
    sugar

4 teaspoons water with 4
    drops hot red pepper
    sauce

2 cups whole, blanched
    almonds

Pepper nuts can be made two weeks in advance and stored in metal containers. You can add or substitute pecan halves for the almonds. Double the recipe if you want to give some as gifts.

Makes 2 cups

Set your oven at 350 degrees. Cover a cookie sheet with aluminum foil and spray it with non-stick spray.

Mix the pepper and salt in a bowl and set aside.

Melt the butter in a large skillet and add the sugar and water infused with hot red pepper sauce. Stir in the nuts and cook until the sauce starts to thicken and is golden brown.

Spread the nuts on the prepared cookie sheet. Sprinkle with the pepper mixture, turning to coat evenly. Make sure the nuts don't stick together.

Bake for 10 minutes. Cool and store in an airtight container.

Cauldron of Clam Chowder

12 chowder clams (4 to 5
   inches across), or 18
   cherrystone clams (2
   inches across), scrubbed

1 cup water

2 tablespoons olive oil or
   butter

4 ounces salt pork, minced

1 onion, finely chopped

2 stalks celery, with leaves,
   chopped

2 cups bottled clam broth

1 teaspoon celery salt

1 tablespoon Worcestershire
   sauce

1 tablespoon dried thyme
   leaves

½ cup finely chopped parsley

Two 26-ounce boxes
   Parmalat imported
   tomatoes, or two 28-
   ounce cans good-quality
   chopped Italian tomatoes,
   with juices

Freshly ground black pepper
   and red pepper flakes to
   taste

If a guest feels a bit depleted on New Year's Day, a cup of this will get him or her back into the ball game. This is a very traditional recipe from the Northern side of my family.

Serves 8 to 10

Place tightly closed, scrubbed clams in a large soup kettle with the water and steam open. Let cool. Strain the juice if it is sandy, and reserve. Grind the clam meat in your food processor, and reserve.

Heat the olive oil or butter and sauté the salt pork, being sure not to let the pot dry out. Place the pork bits on paper towels to drain.

In the same pot, sauté the onion and celery about 6 minutes, until tender. Add the clams, their reserved juice, the salt pork, and the rest of the ingredients.

Cover the pot and simmer gently for 30 minutes. To keep the soup going all day, place in a Crock-Pot.

Note: Be careful of the salt, as some clams are very, very salty!

Fried Crab with Asian Dipping Sauce

Dipping sauce:

1 cup soy sauce

½ cup dry sherry or mirin (rice
  wine)

2 teaspoons minced fresh
  gingerroot

1 tablespoon lemon juice

Crab:

3 strips bacon

8-ounce container whipped
  cream cheese

¼ cup bottled chili sauce

1 cup soft bread crumbs

½ cup mayonnaise

1 teaspoon Dijon-style mustard

Juice of 1 lime

1 egg, lightly beaten

1 pound lump crabmeat, either
  blue crab, Dungeness, or
  snow crab

Salt and pepper to taste

Crispy coating:

1 cup dry bread crumbs to roll
  the crabs in

½ cup all-purpose flour

½ cup cornmeal

1 teaspoon baking powder

These crunchy delights are easy to make in advance, then reheat when your guests arrive.

Makes 24 crab cakes slightly larger than marbles

Whisk all dipping sauce ingredients together and set aside.

Cook the bacon until crisp, and set aside on paper towels. When cool enough to handle, crumble it finely.

In a bowl, mix the rest of the crab ingredients. Don't forget the bacon!

Using a clean grocery-sized plastic bag, mix the coating ingredients together and shake to blend.

Form nice balls using the crab mixture and place in the bag, moving gently from side to side to coat.

Pour 2 inches of canola oil into a larger, deep frying pan or a FryDaddy. Bring the oil to 350 degrees, add the crab balls a few at a time, turn after 15 seconds, and fry until golden. Remove to paper towels to drain.

Store and reheat in the oven just before serving with the dipping sauce.

Deviled Pullet Eggs with Caviar

8 eggs, boiled, run under cold water, cracked, and peeled

Garnish of ¼ teaspoon salmon roe per egg (salty, so consider when salting eggs)

Filling:

Yolks from 8 hard-cooked eggs

½ cup mayonnaise

1 tablespoon butter, at room temperature

1 teaspoon celery salt

1 shallot, cut up

1 teaspoon Dijon-style mustard, or to taste

1 teaspoon freshly ground white pepper

1 teaspoon hot red pepper sauce, or to taste

If you can't get pullet eggs, use the smallest ones you can find. I always make the filling in my food processor so it's silky smooth!

Makes 8

Whirl all the filling ingredients in the bowl of your food processor until very smooth.

Stuff the filling into the egg whites.

Garnish with the salmon roe.

Spinach and Country Ham Quiche

Dough for a 1-crust pie, your
own, refrigerated, or
frozen

4 large eggs

1½ cups light cream

1 cup shredded Muenster
cheese

10-ounce box frozen
chopped spinach,
thawed, excess water
squeezed out

1 cup finely chopped
Virginia or Smithfield ham

2 shallots, minced

¼ teaspoon ground nutmeg

Salt (be careful of the
quantity—the ham is
salty)

Freshly ground black pepper
to taste

You've tried it in the store, now try the real thing. This is such a wonderful combination—a really easy recipe and, yes, real men do eat quiche!

Serves 8

Spray a 9- or 10-inch pie pan with nonstick spray, then fit pie shell into pan.

Set your oven at 400 degrees.

Beat the eggs and cream together. Stir in the rest of the ingredients.

Pour into the pie shell and bake for 15 minutes at 400 degrees, then reduce the heat to 325 degrees and bake for another 45 minutes, or until set. Serve the quiche warm or at room temperature.

Grilled "Lollipops" of Lamb

12 baby rib lamb chops,
    bones trimmed of fat and
    gristle
Salt and pepper to sprinkle
    on the chops

Coating:

¾ stick butter, at room
    temperature
Juice and zest of ½ lemon
1 teaspoon dried mint,
    crumbled, or 1 tablespoon
    chopped fresh mint
1 tablespoon dried lavender
    flowers

These rib lamb chops equal about one nice bite each! They will be very tasty from the coating and absolutely succulent.

Serves 2 to 3
per person as a starter

Sprinkle the chops with salt and pepper.

Set your grill on high gas flame or hot coals.

Mix the coating ingredients and spread on the chops. Grill for 1 to 2 minutes per side.

BIG DADDY LOWDOWN

What Cuts of Veal, Pork, and Lamb are Best for Grilling?

Chops of all three are the best. Remember to go for thicker cuts.

Ring of Fire—Hot Bloody Mary Aspic Ring Filled with Mojo Shrimp

1 pound shrimp, cooked, peeled, and cleaned

1½ cups mojo sauce, your own or bottled

3 envelopes unflavored gelatin

½ cup cold water

1 quart plus 1 cup tomato juice

Juice of 2 limes

1 tablespoon hot red pepper sauce, more to taste

1 tablespoon bottled horseradish

1 tablespoon Worcestershire sauce

1 tablespoon celery salt

This is a very spicy buffet presentation that is made even more delicious with the shrimp.

Serves 8 to 10

Mix the shrimp with the mojo sauce in a large bowl. Cover and refrigerate.

Prepare a 1½-quart ring mold with nonstick spray.

Place the gelatin and water in the jar of your blender. Let the gelatin soften for 5 minutes.

Heat half of the tomato juice to a simmer, then with the motor on low pour half of it into your blender. Add the rest of the ingredients, continuing to spin on low. Pour into the prepared mold and chill for at least 3 hours, or until the gelatin is stiff.

Turn out onto a platter, fill the center, and surround the ring with shrimp.

Note: If you don't care for mojo, use mayonnaise spiced with hot red pepper sauce.

Whole Roast Filet Mignon

4½- to 5-pound whole filet
mignon, fat removed and
tail tucked under

Salt and pepper to sprinkle
on the roast

2 tablespoons butter, at room
temperature

2 tablespoons prepared
mustard

2 tablespoons all-purpose
flour

You can fire-roast this on the grill, or do it in the oven. Make sure it's very well trimmed, as you don't need the extra fat. Have a pan ready to catch the juices.

Serves 10 to 12

Let the roast stand for 30 minutes before cooking. Sprinkle with salt and pepper.

Set your grill or oven at 450 degrees.

Make a paste of the butter, mustard, and flour. Spread it on the roast.

Sear the filet and then roast it at 400 degrees for 45 minutes. Let the meat rest for 10 minutes before carving.

BIG DADDY LOWDOWN

Which Cuts of Beef Are the Most Flavorful?

Rib-eye steak
New York strip
Porterhouse
T-bone

Whole Roast Country Ham

15- to 17-pound country ham, either smoked or salt-sugar cured

2 cups pineapple juice

½ cup packed brown sugar

1 bag cherry wood chips (soaked in apple juice)

Some people always soak or boil country ham prior to cooking to cut down on the salt, and this is definitely recommended. Be sure to check out the step-by-step demonstration for this recipe on the DVD.

Serves 40 to 50

Remove the outer burlap bag or paper and soak the ham overnight in a bucket of water.

Submerge wood chips in apple juice about one hour before cooking. Drain and place chips in an 8½x6-inch aluminum drip pan.

Remove ham from the water and place in a disposable aluminum roasting pan (size will vary depending on the ham), lined with aluminum foil. Wrap ham entirely in foil.

Place the tray of wood chips over the middle burner of your gas grill, on top of the flavor bars (if you have a two-burner grill, place on either side). Set the two outside burners to medium-high and place ham over the chips. (Ignite only the burner opposite the wood chips on a two-burner grill.) Set electric thermometer to 130 degrees.

Mix pineapple juice and brown sugar in a saucepan. Bring to a boil.

Remove ham from the grill once it reaches 130 degrees, and carefully remove foil. Place the ham back on the grill and baste with the pineapple juice mixture. Cook until temperature reaches an internal temperature of 150 degrees, as recommended by the ham producers. The U.S. government recommends 180 degrees, which may dry out the ham. Total cooking time will be 10 to 12 minutes per pound.

BIG DADDY LOWDOWN

What a Ham

The older the ham, the stronger it will be. A country ham is also the American version of prosciutto, only it's much cheaper. Today, you can get spiral cut, ready to heat and serve. You can also buy pre-cooked spiral-sliced hams, ready to heat and eat. Call the National Country Ham Association (800-820-4426) for information on country hams.

Grilled Belgian Endive with Lemon Dressing

10 large Belgian endives,
    halved

Lemon dressing:

1 lemon, cut in small pieces

1½ cups olive oil

2 tablespoons minced chives

2 tablespoons minced fresh
    basil leaves, or 1
    teaspoon dried basil,
    crumbled

Salt and pepper to taste

This is somewhere between a hot vegetable and a salad.

Serves 10 to 12

Bring the dressing ingredients to a boil. Cover and simmer for 20 minutes. Strain and reserve.

Set your grill on high. Place the endive halves on the grill cut side down. Broil for 1 minute. Turn, drizzle with the dressing, and grill for 30 seconds. Serve warm with extra dressing.

A nice presentation includes finely chopped radicchio lettuce, watercress, or arugula.

Iceberg Lettuce Wedges with Warm Prosciutto and Roquefort Dressing

2 heads iceberg lettuce,
    ends and outside leaves
    trimmed, cut in sixths

Dressing:

8 ounces Roquefort cheese,
    crumbled

1 teaspoon lemon juice

Freshly ground black pepper
    to taste

½ cup minced prosciutto ham

The lettuce is cool, crisp, and buttery in flavor, while the dressing is warm and melting.

Serves 12

Arrange the lettuce decoratively on a platter.

Warm the cheese with the lemon juice.

When the cheese melts, spoon it over the wedges of lettuce.

Sprinkle with black pepper and prosciutto ham and serve.

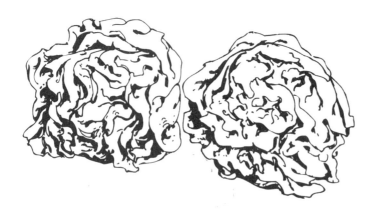

Vermont Cheddar Scalloped Potatoes with Bacon and Onions

6 slices bacon, crumbled

1 large white onion

6 Idaho or Yukon gold
   potatoes

Plenty of freshly ground
   black pepper

4 ounces Vermont sharp
   cheddar cheese, coarsely
   grated

1 cup dry bread crumbs

2 cups whole milk

1 stick butter

This is good, old-fashioned comfort food for the chilly day after the night before.

Serves 12

Fry the bacon until crisp, drain on paper towels, and crumble. Set aside.

Slice the onion paper thin. Peel the potatoes and, using a mandolin, slice thinly.

Prepare a 9x13-inch glass lasagna dish with nonstick spray.

Place a layer of onions and potatoes on the bottom. Sprinkle with crumbled bacon, grind on the pepper, and sprinkle with cheese and bread crumbs.

Continue to layer the ingredients. On the top, pour on milk. Add bread crumbs; dot with butter.

Bake at 325 degrees for 60 to 75 minutes. Keep warm for the duration of your party.

Note: You can use chopped country ham instead of bacon.

Old-Fashioned Apple Crisp with Pears and Dried Cranberries

Topping:

1 stick butter, at room
   temperature

½ cup packed brown sugar

1 cup rolled oats

1 cup all-purpose flour

1 teaspoon ground cinnamon

1 teaspoon salt

1 cup chopped pecans

½ cup chopped walnuts

½ cup chopped hazelnuts

Fruit:

1 cup dried cranberries (or
   raisins) soaked in ¾ cup
   warm water for 20
   minutes

7 apples, peeled, cored, and
   sliced

4 pears, peeled, cored, and
   sliced

½ cup white sugar

2 tablespoons orange zest

1 tablespoon ground
   cinnamon

This is a takeoff on an old favorite with plenty of winter flavors and a very crisp and nutty topping. It's best served warm with some vanilla ice cream melting on the top.

Serves 10

Using your fingers or a pastry blender, work all of the topping ingredients together until mixture looks like a crumbly, chunky paste. Set aside.

Set your oven at 350 degrees.

Generously butter a 9x13-inch glass baking dish, or prepare with nonstick spray.

Pile in the fruits. Sprinkle with the sugar, orange zest, and cinnamon.

Dot the fruit with the topping, spreading as evenly as possible.

Bake for 40 to 50 minutes, until the fruits are sizzling and the topping is brown.

Winter Fruit Compote— Macerated Mangoes, Bananas, and Pineapple with Pomegranate Glaze

Glaze:

3 cups pomegranate juice

Juice of ½ lime

4 ounces orange Curacao

2 pineapples, cleaned, cored, and cut in pieces

3 firm-ripe mangoes, peeled, cored, and diced

2 bananas, peeled and sliced

2 tablespoons lemon juice

2 oranges, peeled and sections removed

Garnish: toasted coconut chips, toasted macadamia or hazelnuts, sprigs of fresh mint, raspberry liqueur or citron vodka, lime, orange, or lemon sorbet (sprinkle, spritz, or scoop on top of compote)

This is really refreshing on the day after the night before. It makes your guests feel as healthy as they will this day!

Serves 10 to 12

Boil the pomegranate juice down to 2 cups.

Add the lime juice and Curacao. Set aside.

Prepare the fruits, adding lemon juice to the bananas so they won't turn brown.

Place the fruits in a large bowl and pour the reserved glaze over the fruits, mixing gently.

You can serve lemon or lime sorbet on the side if you want an extra bit of festivity.

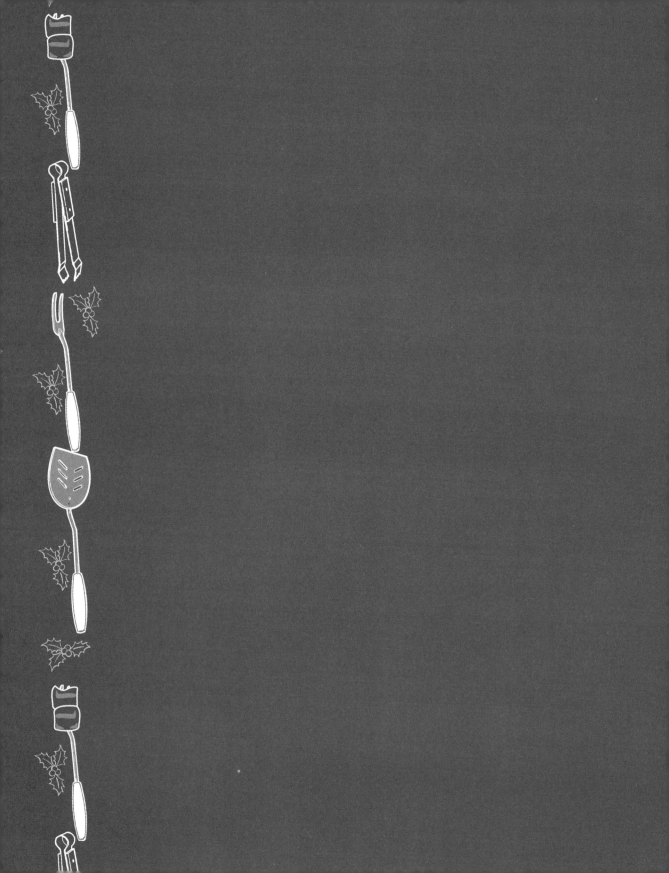

Chapter 6

Special Feasts and Sides

America is the ultimate melting pot, and we mean that literally. The blending of cultures from around the world, along with their flavors and tastes, has created a unique experience in international cuisine. Add to that the regional specialties and varieties, and you've got a limitless selection of feasts to work with.

The Irish never considered this, but did you know the best corned beef on St. Paddy's Day is prepared on the grill? And why not extol the Italian heritage on Columbus Day with such dishes as pasta with shrimp, cockles and mussels, or grilled Italian sausage served with roasted red peppers on garlic bruschetta?

Memorial Day is the World Series of grilling, the opening salvo in the summer of outdoor fun. May we recommend lobster on the grill to get the season off right?

Here are some great party favorites to meet the demand on great holidays, from America, the great culinary melting pot. If you can think of a few more holidays, you can come up with exciting and different dishes to grill for them.

MEMORIAL DAY
Grilled Lobsters

1 lobster (1½ to 2 pounds) per
    person
½ stick butter per person
½ lemon, cut in wedges, per
    person

For the unofficial kickoff of the summer, serving lobsters on your deck or patio makes a perfect start. If it gets chilly, or rains, the lobsters still taste great! Lobster lovers generally make a sauce with melted butter and lemon juice. As soon as the lobsters are red on both sides, they are done.

Set your grill at about 400 degrees. Make sure the lobster is wiggling; never eat a dead lobster. Rinse the lobster in cold water, and carefully remove the bands on the claws, as they could make a nasty smell when on the grill.

Melt the butter.

Place the lobster belly side up on the grill and close the lid. Roast it for 6 to 8 minutes and turn it. Give it another 6 to 8 minutes. Cool slightly.

When cool enough to handle, split the lobster down the middle from the underside of the thorax and through the tail. Remove the "dead man," or intestine.

Set up an "elegant tablecloth" of newspapers. Use lots of paper napkins and dig in! Serve the butter in small bowls and pass the lemon wedges around.

COLUMBUS DAY
Pasta with Grilled Whole Clams and Shrimp in Red Sauce

Sauce:

2 tablespoons olive oil

4 cloves garlic, minced

½ red onion, chopped

1 teaspoon dried oregano
   leaves, or 1 tablespoon
   fresh oregano

1 teaspoon dried basil
   leaves

½ cup dry red wine

2½ cups fresh plum tomato
   puree (fresh tomatoes
   rinsed and whirled in the
   blender)

½ cup Italian flat-leaf parsley

Pinch white sugar

Salt and freshly ground
   black pepper to taste

Red pepper flakes to taste

Pasta and seafood:

1 pound linguini

24 littleneck clams,
   scrubbed and tightly
   closed

24 large shrimp, peeled and
   deveined

We always eat some Italian food on Columbus Day. And good seafood is such a part of that cuisine. You also should be able to get great farm stand tomatoes for your sauce.

Serves 6

Heat the olive oil in a large saucepot over medium-low flame.

Add the garlic and red onion and cook about 6 to 8 minutes, until translucent.

Slowly add the rest of the sauce ingredients, stirring. Reduce heat, cover, and simmer for at least 30 minutes.

Set the fire to hot. Start a large pot of salted water for the pasta.

After the sauce has cooked, place the clams on the grill until they just start to open. Add them to the sauce.

Grill the shrimp for 30 seconds per side and add them to the sauce.

When the pasta is done, drain and mix into the pot with the sauce and seafood.

Serve in large bowls with an extra bowl on hand for the shells.

ST. PATRICK'S DAY
Leek and Potato Soup Garnished with Irish Bacon

Bacon:
½ pound Irish bacon, thickly
   sliced

Soup:
1 stick butter (You could use
   olive oil but butter is truly
   Irish.)

4 onions, chopped

4 leeks, white part only,
   chopped, rinsed to
   remove sand

4 potatoes, peeled and
   chopped

1 quart rich chicken broth

1½ cups whole milk

1 cup heavy or whipping
   cream

½ cup fresh watercress,
   rinsed and finely chopped

¼ cup fresh parsley, rinsed
   and finely chopped

Salt and pepper to taste

In Ireland, they do not eat corned beef and cabbage on St. Patrick's Day; that's actually a New England thing. They eat Irish bacon, which is smoked loin of pork and very delicious indeed. This soup makes a fantastic lunch and is delightfully green!

Serves 6 to 8

Set your grill on medium-high. Place the bacon over the coals or flame and cook until crisp, turning frequently.

Drain and chop bacon. Set aside.

Melt the butter and add the onions and leeks. Sauté until softened. Add the potatoes and chicken broth. Simmer, covered, over low heat until the potatoes are soft.

Stir in the milk, cream, herbs, and spices.

Blend with a wand blender or pulse in the bowl of your food processor. Don't overmix or the potatoes will get gluey.

Reheat when ready to serve and garnish each bowl with bacon.

ROSH HASHANAH
Smoked Brisket

7- to 8-pound brisket of beef

Rub and mop:

1 can rich, golden beer, such as Heineken

2 Scotch bonnet chilies, minced

¾ cup cider vinegar or simple white vinegar

¼ cup Worcestershire sauce

2 tablespoons dark brown sugar

To finish making the mop:

½ of the mixture listed above

1 cup bottled barbecue sauce

¼ cup water

2 tablespoons chili powder (for a very hot mop, use more—or add less chili powder to make it milder)

½ teaspoon freshly ground black pepper

This is as Western as it is Jewish! The brisket is one of the very special cuts that takes an expert to prepare. This recipe is dedicated to Texan Kinky Friedman! You will need a smoker, a rub, and a "mop," a basting liquid that gets mopped on the beef.

Serves 12 to 14

Mix the rub and mop ingredients together in a bowl. Rub half of it over the meat and cover. Refrigerate the meat overnight.

Mix the remaining ingredients together. Set ½ cup aside in a separate bowl, covered, to use in sauce, and keep the rest warm for basting the beef.

Use natural wood charcoal (no artificial starters!) and your favorite flavor wood chips, either mesquite or hickory, presoaking the chips for 2 hours. Start the fire in your smoker. When it reaches 225 degrees, cook the beef fat side up. Add more charcoal and damp chips every 1 to 2 hours.

Mop the beef whenever you open the smoker to add charcoal and chips.

Smoke the beef for 12 to 14 hours. Turn fat side down for the last hour of smoking. Let the meat rest for 15 minutes before carving. Add more sauce, and serve with fixin's!

Mix the reserved half-cup of mop with more barbecue sauce, warm, and serve it on the side.

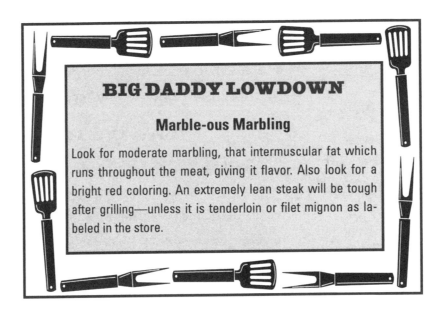

BIG DADDY LOWDOWN

Marble-ous Marbling

Look for moderate marbling, that intermuscular fat which runs throughout the meat, giving it flavor. Also look for a bright red coloring. An extremely lean steak will be tough after grilling—unless it is tenderloin or filet mignon as labeled in the store.

EID
Lamb Kabobs

Marinade:

½ cup olive oil

¼ cup lemon juice

1 teaspoon ground coriander

½ teaspoon ground cumin

1 teaspoon chili oil or 1 teaspoon harissa (chili paste)

4 cloves garlic, chopped

½ onion, chopped

Kabobs:

4 pounds lamb, from the leg

Salt and pepper to sprinkle on the lamb

4 sweet red bell peppers, cored, seeded, and cut in chunks

10 baby onions, peeled

16 to 20 wooden skewers, soaked in water for at least 1 hour

Derived from Eid, an Islamic feast, these recipes are very simple and require only a few special spices. The lamb kabobs are tender and delicious. The rice pudding is as good as it gets (recipe follows).

Serves 8 to 10

Cut the lamb into 2-inch chunks.

Salt and pepper the lamb. Mix the marinade ingredients together.

Place the lamb in a bowl and add the marinade, tossing lamb to coat.

Thread lamb, pepper, and onion on skewers.

Set your grill at 400 degrees. Sear lamb on each side. Close lid and fire-roast for about 5 minutes per side.

Serve with vegetables.

Rice and Carrot Pudding

10 cups whole milk

5 pounds carrots, peeled and
    grated

1 cup basmati rice

Salt to taste

1 cup white sugar

½ teaspoon ground
    cardamom

This is a traditional Eastern dessert. Our Pakistani friend makes it and it's very delicious.

Serves 10 to 14

Bring the milk to a boil. Add the carrots. Stir in the rice, salt, and sugar. Stir, simmering, until thickened, about 40 minutes (a great project to get the kids involved in!). Toward the end of the cooking, add the cardamom.

BASTILLE DAY
Individual Cod and Potato Soufflés

2 pounds fresh codfish
fillets, skinned

Juice of ½ lemon

4 large Idaho potatoes,
peeled and boiled

½ cup milk

1 stick butter

Salt and pepper to taste

6 eggs, separated

The day the Bastille was stormed, liberating France symbolically, is cause for high celebrating. People feast in France, and around the globe, people of French heritage raise their native flag, and usually a glass or two. This dish is fine as an appetizer, or a celebratory lunch with a green salad and soup for a starter, especially on July 14, Bastille Day.

Serves 10

Set your oven at 400 degrees.

Rinse the fish, checking for bones. Poach it in simmering water with lemon juice for about 10 minutes, or until it flakes.

In a large bowl, mash the boiled potatoes with milk and plenty of butter. Add salt and pepper to taste.

Using a pancake turner or rubber spatula, add the fish and turn from the bottom to the top, making a "fold." (This form of blending keeps things fluffed up. If you stir, you'll decrease the volume of the food. The same is true with adding egg whites. Just give the mixture a gentle turning in with the rubber spatula and it will stay puffy.)

Whip the egg whites until stiff. Stir 3 of the yolks into the mixture of fish and potatoes. Fold in the egg whites.

Prepare ten 1-cup soufflé dishes or two 6-cup soufflé dishes with nonstick spray. Place on a cookie sheet in the oven and bake for 30 minutes, until nicely puffed.

Ratatouille Made with Grilled Vegetables

2 red bell peppers

4 baby eggplants, sliced
lengthwise

5 large zucchini, cut in half

¼ cup olive oil

2 cloves garlic, chopped

4 onions, chopped

2 cups chopped fresh
tomatoes

Salt and freshly ground
black pepper

½ cup fresh basil leaves,
chopped and loosely
packed

2 tablespoons fresh
rosemary, stripped
from stem

½ cup Italian flat-leaf
parsley, chopped

This classic French vegetable dish can be served hot or at room temperature. It's very delicious and adapts well as a side with any fish, meat, or poultry. It's also wonderful on a thinly sliced baguette.

Serves 6 as a side dish, 10 as an hors d'oeuvre

Cut the peppers in half, remove the seeds, and stem. Char on the grill until the skins are blackened. Place in a paper or plastic bag. This will make the skin come off easily. When cool enough to handle, remove the skin, chop, and set aside.

Place the eggplants on the grill flesh side down and skin up. Roast about 5 minutes, until softened, then remove, cut in small pieces, and set aside.

Cut zucchini into chunks and cook on grill until skin is golden.

Heat the olive oil and sauté the garlic and onions until just softened. Add the tomatoes and bring to a boil. Add the skinned peppers and chopped eggplant to the pan. Sprinkle with salt and pepper. Stir in the chopped herbs and serve.

LABOR DAY
Sirloin Burgers Stuffed
with Cheese and Chilies

2 portobello mushrooms (6-inch diameter)

½ cup of your favorite Italian dressing

2 pounds ground sirloin

1 teaspoon salt

Pepper to taste

2 tablespoons steak sauce

2 tablespoons cored, seeded, and minced jalapeño pepper

½ cup crumbled Gorgonzola cheese

6 of your favorite burger rolls

Fixin's of onions, tomato, lettuce, ketchup, mustard, etc.

Labor Day, to honor the working man and woman, is the unofficial end of summer. It's a perfect time to invite a lot of people and grill away a lazy afternoon. Here's one of our favorite holiday recipes.

Serves 6

Preheat the grill to 400 degrees.

Brush off the mushrooms and remove stems. Put the whole mushrooms in a plastic bag with the dressing, seal, and marinate for at least 1 hour.

Mix the sirloin, salt, pepper, steak sauce, and jalapeño pepper together.

Make 12 thin patties. Sprinkle 6 with cheese, then use the other 6 patties to top, pressing the edges together. Grill over hot coals to desired level of doneness. Toast the rolls on the grill.

Cook mushrooms on grill for about 2 ½ minutes per side. Place on a serving platter and use to top burgers.

Serve with all of the fixin's and plenty of beer.

CHINESE NEW YEAR
Roast Suckling Pig for Good Luck

10- to 12-pound suckling pig

Salt and pepper

½ cup peanut oil

1 tablespoon Chinese five-
spice powder

1 small red apple

During the Chinese New Year celebration, every dish has significance. Our dear Chinese friend orders the suckling pig for her New Year's party from Chinatown. It's cooked and ready to take home, warm up, and serve. Checking with other chefs, a good pig can be ordered fresh and delivered on ice to your home. Be careful to get a small one, 10 to 15 pounds.

Serves 16 to 20

Set your grill at 350 degrees or get the coals to white-hot.

Rinse the pig and pat it dry. Put a piece of wood in its mouth to brace it open so that you can add the apple after it's cooked.

Sprinkle the pig with salt and pepper, in and out. Rub with peanut oil. Rub with five-spice powder. Truss the legs underneath the pig and make a few shallow knife slits along the back to let the fat run out.

Roast for about 3 hours, or until the internal temperature reaches 155 degrees. Let the meat rest for 20 minutes, covered. Carve and serve with the apple in its mouth. The skin should be crispy and the meat succulent.

Stuffed Mushrooms for Fertility

30 white mushrooms, stems
removed and minced

½ cup peanut oil

2 tablespoons sesame seed
oil

6 scallions, chopped

1 tablespoon minced fresh
gingerroot

2 cloves garlic, minced

1½ cups cooked white rice

4 tablespoons soy sauce

4 tablespoons sherry

Freshly ground black pepper
or red pepper flakes to
taste

This is another traditional Chinese New Year's dish. The mushroom symbolizes the womb and the stuffing, well, you can figure it out yourself.

Makes 30 small, stuffed button mushrooms

Preheat the oven, or the grill to indirect heat at 300 degrees. Cover a cookie sheet with aluminum foil and prepare with nonstick spray. Place mushroom caps on cookie sheet. Mince stems and set aside.

Heat the peanut oil and mix in the sesame oil. Add the scallions, ginger, and garlic and sauté for 6 minutes over low flame, stirring constantly. Mix in the rest of the ingredients, including minced mushroom stems.

Using a teaspoon, mound the filling into the caps, bake for 10 minutes, and serve hot!

Long Noodles for a Long Life!

1 cup peanut oil

¼ cup sesame seed oil

10 scallions, minced

2 cups chopped Chinese or
Napa cabbage

1 large onion, chopped

4 cloves garlic, chopped

1 cup soy sauce (light soy is
fine)

2 boxes rice noodles or
linguini, cooked to
package directions

Black or red pepper to taste

Another very auspicious traditional dish to make you feel good and optimistic is the big bowl of noodles on the side. Many supermarkets have long Asian rice noodles; if you can't find them, linguini is just fine! Everyone takes three or four strands for a long life!

Serves 20

Warm the oil in a very large pan, and add the vegetables. Sauté for 6 to 8 minutes. Stir in the rest of the ingredients, being sure to coat all of the noodles.

Serve in a decorative bowl and live well!

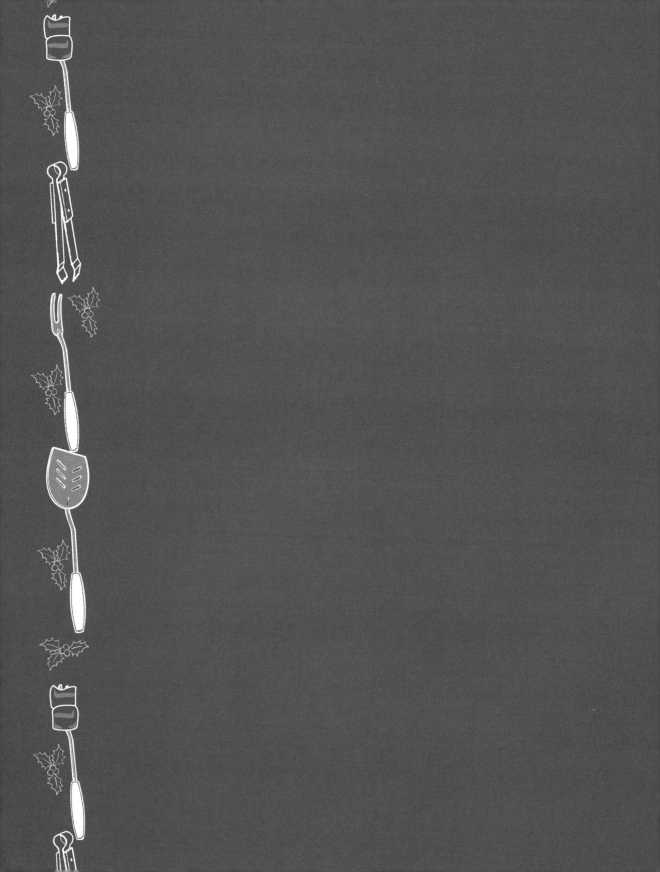

Chapter 7

Year-Round Pleasures: Every Day's a Holiday— Feasts and Sides

Yeah, yeah, sure, sure, you've heard that before: every day's a holiday. Well, the good news for you glass-half-full people is that every day is a holiday. You've got a birthday, an anniversary, a christening, a bris—and for you glass-half-empty people, you can turn every day into a holiday with a fantastic grilling party.

You don't have to look at the calendar to have a great grilling feast. Here are some dishes that can be prepared quickly to provide a festive atmosphere for your family and friends. We're talking grilled veal chops, roast chicken, and Philly-style cheesesteak sandwiches. For those of you who have never tried them, explanation is impossible. For those who have, no further promotion is needed! Finish your meal with grilled mini pizzas with the toppings of your choice, skewered veggies, or put your jar of sauerkraut on steroids and have the best-tasting kraut of your life. These are economical and easy recipes that can be done after a day at the quarry, simple fare that everyone in the family will enjoy. With a little help from your friends and a couple of brewskis, you can even have the game on the whole time. Who needs to go out to the local hangout when the fun is right in your own backyard?

Philadelphia-Style Cheesesteak Sandwiches

½ stick unsalted butter

1 large white onion, thinly sliced

Four 6-ounce hanger or cube steaks, or two 12-ounce filets mignons

8 slices very good bread or 4 hoagie (Philly talk for hero or submarine) rolls

Salt and pepper to taste

Worcestershire sauce to taste

8 slices really good American cheese, such as Land O'Lakes, or try Velveeta

If your local store does not have hanger steak, you can use cube steaks, or get really fancy with some filet mignon! The better the steak, the more luscious the sandwich. You need some really good bread to do this one justice. Try a big, round loaf of Tuscan bread. It's not exactly a Philly thing, but good, and easy to make big slices!

Serves 4

Set your grill at 400 degrees.

Melt the butter and sauté the onion until very limp and golden.

In a separate pan, sear the steaks on both sides. If you are using nice thick filets, sear and reduce flame to cook until rare-to-medium all the way through. Cut the filet thin; cube or hanger steaks can just go on the rolls.

Toast the bread or rolls. Place a steak or pieces of sliced steak on each, and sprinkle with the salt, pepper, and Worcestershire. Mound with the onion and cover the top with cheese. Put back on the grill until the cheese melts. Yum!

Grilled Veal Chops

6 large loin veal chops (6 to 8
  ounces each and 2 inches
  thick)

Sauce:
¾ stick butter
2 tablespoons coarse-
  grained mustard
2 tablespoons dried
  rosemary leaves, or 3
  tablespoons rosemary, if
  fresh, plus a few sprigs to
  put into the fire to
  perfume the chops
6 tablespoons grated
  Parmesan cheese
2 teaspoons red pepper
  flakes, or to taste

Once we were at a fancy restaurant and I ordered a veal chop. When dinner arrived I thought someone had fixed me a snowshoe! It was pounded and extended until it was huge! Loin veal chops are expensive and wonderful. Spread with the sauce just before you finish cooking them, and you'll find everyone salivating like a pack of hungry wolves.

Serves 6

Melt the butter, stir in the rest of the sauce ingredients, and set aside.

Set your grill at 450 degrees and sear chops. Turn down the flame or put over indirect heat and cook for 5 minutes per side for rare.

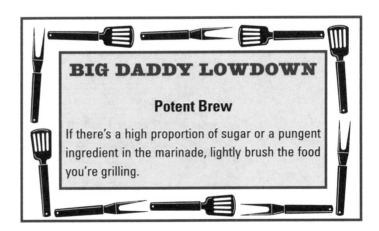

BIG DADDY LOWDOWN

Potent Brew

If there's a high proportion of sugar or a pungent ingredient in the marinade, lightly brush the food you're grilling.

When the chops are nearly done, spread the sauce on one side, and turn the chops so that side is down. Spread the sauce on the other side. When the chops are golden, place on a warm platter, cover, and let rest for 10 minutes (the meat will continue to cook). Serve with pasta, mashed potatoes, or any vegetable.

The Best Roast Chicken

2 small chickens (about 3
  pounds each)
Salt and pepper
1 stick butter, at room
  temperature
½ cup parsley
2 tablespoons fresh thyme
2 oranges, peeled and cut in
  chunks, seeds removed
4 strips bacon
Mesquite chips, soaked in
  water, to add flavor to the
  fire

Fire-roasted chicken is wonderful—add some mesquite chips to the fire and be sure to keep the heat even. You can use any herbs you really like, including thyme, sage, rosemary, or parsley. Parsley goes with everything.

Serves 6 to 8

Set your grill at 400 degrees.

Rinse the chickens and pat dry with paper towels. Sprinkle inside and out with salt and pepper.

Mix the softened butter with the parsley, thyme, and more salt and pepper and tease under the chicken skin, being careful not to tear the skin.

Place the oranges inside the chicken cavities with an extra sprig of thyme. Truss the legs closed and arrange the bacon over the top of the breasts.

Place the chickens in a large aluminum roasting pan and roast them for 35 minutes, or until the interior temperature is 150 degrees. Remove the bacon after 20 minutes. Reduce heat to 325 degrees and cook for another half hour, for a total of 60 to 65 minutes. Baste while cooking.

Let the chickens rest for 20 minutes before carving.

Wrigley Red Hots

2 hot dogs per person

2 poppy-seed rolls per
person

Chopped onion

Yellow mustard

Sweet pickle relish

Slices of fresh tomato

Pickle spears

Hot pepper sauce

Dash of celery salt per dog

These Vienna beef dogs are loaded with greenery!

Grill the dogs to your liking.

Toast the rolls.

Load 'em up with goodies. Eat!

Bronx Bomber Kosher Franks with Sauerkraut and Mustard

2 franks per person

2 fresh-baked rolls per person

¼ cup sauerkraut, warmed, per person

Deli mustard—brown is best

Some vendors boil their franks, others grill them. Either way, when you're in New York, you'll most likely get a Hebrew National frank. These are garlicky and good.

Grill the franks.

Toast the rolls.

Heat the sauerkraut.

Load 'em up with mustard on top!

Tuna Steaks with Coarse-Ground Mustard and Lemon-Flavored Rum

4 tuna steaks, about 6
   ounces each

½ cup lemon-flavored rum

½ cup mustard seeds,
   crushed with a mortar
   and pestle

Salt to taste

This is a taste of the islands, very special and piquant!

Serves 4

Rinse the fish, and pat dry with paper towels.

Combine the rum, mustard seeds, and salt until well mixed.

Spread on both sides of the tuna steaks.

Grill for 4 minutes per side for medium-rare.

BIG DADDY LOWDOWN

And What Do You Drink with Fish?

Very fruity wines can take the heat. For fish, serve Vouvray or Chenin Blanc. For beef, try a California Zinfandel. Poultry and pork will go with either.

South African Lobster Tail Stuffed with Snail Butter

Snail butter:

¾ stick butter, at room
temperature

6 teaspoons minced fresh
parsley

6 cloves garlic, minced

18 frozen South African
lobster tails, defrosted

Snail butter is basically very garlicky butter that works well with these tender little delights. The lobster tails are quite small and expensive too. Figure on three per person with a couple of sides.

Serves 6

You'll need a very hot grill to do these right. Do not overcook.

Mash the butter, parsley, and garlic together.

Split open the underside of the tails with a sharp knife, but don't cut all the way through.

Spoon the butter into the split. Cook split side up for 3 to 4 minutes.

Skewered Vegetables

12 skewers, soaked in water
    for at least 1 hour

3 yellow bell peppers, cored,
    seeded, and cut in chunks

3 small zucchini, cut in
    chunks

24 cherry tomatoes

12 cremini mushrooms

¾ cup olive oil

½ cup minced mint

Salt and pepper to taste

Extra mint, for garnish

When vegetables have been fire-roasted they take on a special flavor. And, adding a Sicilian touch of mint and olive oil makes them lush.

Serves 6

Thread the skewers, alternating vegetables on each.

Mix the olive oil, mint, salt, and pepper. Brush on the vegetables.

Grill over medium flame or coals until hot and just a bit wilted. This will take 8 to 10 minutes per side.

Sprinkle with extra mint and serve as a side dish, over rice, or with pasta.

BIG DADDY LOWDOWN

Don't Let Your Veggies Get All Wet

Marinate vegetables just before grilling to avoid making them soggy.

Grilled Mini Pizzas with Greek Olives, Fresh Tomatoes, and Feta Cheese

1 pound pizza dough, rolled thin, cut into four 5- to 6-inch rounds

¼ cup olive oil

1 cup Greek or Italian black olives, pitted, cut up

8 ounces Feta cheese, crumbled

16 cherry or teardrop tomatoes, halved

½ cup capers

4 teaspoons dried oregano leaves

4 tablespoons finely minced fresh basil leaves

Plenty of freshly ground black pepper

½ cup freshly grated Parmesan cheese

(Hold the salt—the saltiness of the cheese and olives should suffice.)

The good news is you can buy pizza dough at your local supermarket or from a pizzeria.

Serves 4

You'll need the grill to be very hot and the pizzas to bake on indirect heat.

When the dough is rolled out, brush it with the olive oil. Sprinkle with the olives, Feta cheese, tomatoes, capers, oregano, basil, and pepper.

Fire-grill the pizzas until they are golden and the cheese has started to melt. Sprinkle with the Parmesan cheese immediately.

Try this with a good red wine and a green salad . . . mmmm.

Stuffed Calzones

1 pound pizza dough, rolled
    thin, cut into four 6-inch
    rounds
¼ cup olive oil
1 pound Italian sausage,
    sweet or hot, fried and
    crumbled
2 roasted red peppers,
    packed in oil, cut in small
    dice
4 ounces fresh mozzarella
    cheese or, even better,
    buffalo mozzarella, thinly
    sliced
1 cup canned artichoke
    hearts, drained and
    chopped

A calzone is like a pizza turnover! Very delicious and very hot inside. Stuffings are limited only by your imagination and taste buds—all very personal. This is just a recommendation—go, Daddy, go!

Serves 4

Set your grill at 375 degrees.

When you've rolled out the pizza dough, sprinkle with the olive oil.

Evenly divide the rest of the ingredients between the calzones, mounding them only on one side of the round.

Fold the plain half over the filled half and press down the edges. (You can use a bit of beaten egg to make sure the edges stay closed.)

Prick the top of each calzone with a fork, and bake for 15 minutes over indirect heat, until golden brown and very hot.

Risotto with Exotic Mushrooms

Mushrooms:

½ stick butter

4 shallots, minced

10 shiitake mushrooms,
    cleaned and chopped

10 small white button
    mushrooms, cleaned and
    chopped

5 small cremini mushrooms

¾ cup beef broth

¼ cup dry red wine

Salt and pepper to taste

Rice:

1 cup basmati or arborio rice

¼ cup olive oil

6 cups chicken broth,
    warmed

Salt and pepper to taste

½ cup grated Parmesan
    cheese

½ cup parsley, washed and
    chopped

The only difficult thing about making risotto is that you have to listen to it, stir it constantly, and keep slowly adding the stock to the pot of rice. However, the creamy, delicious result is well worth the trouble.

Serves 6

Heat the butter in a large saucepan. Stir in the shallots and mushrooms. Cook and stir over low heat until the mushrooms are soft. Add the rest of the ingredients. Set aside while you prepare the rice.

Using a big saucepan, sauté the rice in the oil for 6 minutes.

Stirring, add ½ cup of the warm chicken broth. When the rice hisses, add more and keep stirring. Repeat until all of the broth is gone and the rice is creamy. Add salt and pepper. Stir in the reserved mushrooms. Sprinkle with Parmesan cheese and parsley and serve.

Making Sauerkraut from a Jar
Taste Like You Made It

1 quart sauerkraut in the jar
(better than canned, no
metallic taste)
½ cup cider vinegar or white
vinegar
½ stick butter, melted
1 teaspoon caraway seed,
crushed with a mortar
and pestle
½ teaspoon celery salt
Freshly ground black pepper
to taste

There is no real trick to this, but it's sooo much better than just using it out of the jar.

Makes 1 quart

Drain and rinse the sauerkraut in cold water. Squeeze to remove most of the water.

Add the rest of the ingredients and toss to mix. Serve warm.

Cold Rice Salad with Crunchy Veggies and Wild Sauce

2 cups cooked rice, chilled

2 celery stalks, chopped

½ cup finely chopped sweet onion

2 hot chilis, such as Scotch bonnets or jalapeños, cored, seeded, and minced

10 cherry tomatoes, halved

1 cup chopped leftover roast chicken, ham, or cooked shrimp

4 avocados, halved

Sauce:

1 cup mayonnaise (light is fine)

Juice of ½ lime

1 teaspoon Dijon-style mustard

1 teaspoon curry powder

This is a wonderful way to use leftover ham, chicken, or shrimp.

Serves 4

Toss all but the avocados in a bowl.

Mix the sauce ingredients, and add to the rice mixture. Serve chilled, mounded in avocados.

Chapter 8

Regional Favorites: The Best of Americana

No matter where you are in this great country, there's great eating to be had. And much of it focuses on the grill. Here are some of the wonderful dishes that we've culled from the corners of America, from Yuma, Arizona, to Yarmouth, Massachusetts.

Some of the most renowned barbecue joints include Corky's in Memphis, Tennessee; Carson's in Chicago; Bobby Q's in Westport, Connecticut; The Brick Pit in Mobile, Alabama; Coopers BBQ in Llano, Texas; and anyplace in Kansas City, Missouri. Add to that the dozens, if not hundreds, of tiny BBQ joints (we're partial to Brooks' Bar-B-Q in Oneonta, New York) and you'll be screeching the tires and pulling over to the side of the road.

In fact it's those roadside stands and pits that are the inspiration for this chapter, which brings us to the true essence of American BBQ: open-pit cooking.

Pig roasts are popular all over. We've found five variations on this tradition, with lots of great eating to carry you through a weekend of partying.

The tailgate party is another great tradition at sporting events and campuses everywhere. We know of many friendships, relationships, and babies that were made during the course of such events.

Whether on the East Coast or the West Coast or on waters in between, the clambake allows for the perfect match of fresh seafood and grilled delights.

PIG ROAST WITH ITALIAN SAUCE AND BRUSCHETTA

Pig roasts are popular all over. David McCue, chef/owner of the Wilton Food Company, in Wilton, Connecticut, is a pro at putting on pig roasts! He uses a rotisserie over a slow fire, and a combination of wood and coals, where the coals serve to regulate the fire. "Even a thirty-pound pig is heavy on bone, you'll get about fifteen pounds of meat which will serve about twenty people." He saves trimmings from his apple and cherry trees, which add greatly to the flavor. He also soaks the wood in a bucket of leftover wine. McCue points out that the fire can get too hot, and he's always got a beer in hand when he's roasting a pig so he can pour some on the pig to cool it down. "You get a nice malty scent from the beer!" he says. About regular basting, "The skin cracks and the fat runs out, basting the pig naturally."

To prepare the pig, season the outside with salt, pepper, and herbs to suit the ethnic flavoring. (Rub in 1 tablespoon of lemon zest when roasting the pig with Italian sauce.) Use garlic and oregano inside the pig. Then stuff it with cooked rice, onions, tomatoes, garlic, and scallions seasoned with salt, pepper, and basil. Use chicken wire to keep it together. The chicken wire is ingenious; the pig stays together as the wire forms a net to keep the meat out of the fire.

Splash the pig with beer while it's roasting. The smoke will season the outside of the pig.

The pig is done when the internal temperature reaches 155 degrees. After the pig is roasted, you put out all of your favorite ethnic and regional sauces and sides.

Serve the pig on a platter, carved, with a lemony tomato sauce on the side. Toasted Italian bread and tomato salad go well.

Lemony Tomato Sauce:

½ cup olive oil

2 red onions, finely chopped

4 cloves garlic, finely
    chopped

8 cups chopped fresh plum
    or Roma tomatoes, stem
    ends removed, whirled in
    the jar of your blender

1 cup dry red wine, such as
    Chianti

Juice of 1 lemon

Salt and black pepper to
    taste

1 teaspoon red pepper
    flakes, or to taste

1 teaspoon dried oregano
    leaves

1 cup fresh basil leaves,
    rinsed and torn apart

½ cup parsley, rinsed and
    torn apart

Lemony Tomato Sauce

Heat the oil in a large saucepot. Add the onion and garlic and sauté until soft, but do not brown.

Add the tomatoes, wine, and lemon juice. Sprinkle in salt and black and red pepper.

Finish with the oregano, basil, and parsley. Cover and simmer for 1 hour.

Serve as a sauce with the pig.

Bruschetta

This wonderful side is now very popular. The basic recipe is simply thinly sliced Italian or French bread, rubbed with olive oil and garlic. It's spread with chopped fresh tomatoes and more olive oil, then run under the broiler. To vary, add onion, parsley, chopped garlic, and a pinch of Parmesan cheese to the tomato. When the bread is almost toasted, remove from the oven and sprinkle with shredded mozzarella to finish off.

SOUTHERN-MIDWESTERN PIG ROAST WITH BOURBON BBQ SAUCE AND SOUTHERN SIDES

Serve the pig with corn bread, a wilted spinach salad, and potato salad. While the pig is roasting, make Bourbon BBQ Sauce.

1 stick butter

4 onions, chopped

4 cloves garlic, chopped

2 bottles chili sauce or
   ketchup

2 cups chopped tomatoes,
   fresh are best but canned
   are fine

1 cup packed brown sugar

¼ cup molasses

¼ cup Worcestershire sauce

½ cup white vinegar

Juice of 1 lemon

4 whole cloves

½ cup bourbon

Bourbon BBQ Sauce

Warm the butter in a large pot. Add the onions and garlic. Sauté over low heat until softened.

Add the rest of the ingredients and cover. Cook at a simmer for 2 hours.

Serve on the side with roast pig.

SOUTH/CENTRAL AMERICAN PIG ROAST WITH CHIMICHURRI, GUACAMOLE, AND BLACK BEAN SALAD

After roasting the pig, place it on a platter surrounded with tacos, guacamole, Black Bean Salad, and bottled, or your own, chimichurri sauce. Fried plantain strips make a crunchy counterpoint to the soft pork.

½ cup olive oil

2 red onions, minced

4 cloves garlic, minced

6 tomatillos, peeled and chopped

4 carrots, peeled and grated

1 pint small tomatoes, such as teardrop, halved

Juice of 1 lime

2 tablespoons vinegar

Salt and red pepper sauce to taste

4 cans black beans, rinsed

1 can hearts of palm, rinsed and chopped

Chopped cilantro and scallions, for garnish

Black Bean Salad

Serves 10

Heat the oil in a frying pan, then stir in the onion and garlic. Cook briefly, until crisp-tender.

Place in a large bowl with the rest of the ingredients, except garnishes. Cover and refrigerate for at least 3 hours. Garnish with chopped cilantro and scallions.

CARIBBEAN PIG ROAST WITH JERK SPICES, MANGO SAUCE, AND PEAS AND RICE

When the pig is done, make a sauce with mangoes, oranges, and plenty of commercial jerk spices.

Mango Sauce:

8 ripe mangoes

1 tablespoon grated fresh gingerroot

½ cup packed brown sugar

1 tablespoon jerk spices

Juice of 1 fresh lime

Juice of ½ lemon

2 tablespoons vinegar

Salt and hot red pepper to taste

Peas and Rice:

2 cups rice

1 tablespoon salt

½ cup vegetable oil

3 onions, chopped

2 tablespoons grated fresh gingerroot

4 cloves garlic, chopped

4 hot chili peppers, cored and seeded

2 cans black-eyed peas, rinsed

1 tablespoon jerk seasoning, or to taste

Mango Sauce

Makes 4 cups

Peel and cube mangoes. Mix in a bowl with the rest of the ingredients. Cover and chill. Serve with the pig.

Peas and Rice

A traditional dish in the Caribbean and in the South; the Caribbean version is very spicy!

Serves 10 to 12

Cook the rice in 4 cups of salted water.

Heat the vegetable oil and sauté the onion, ginger, garlic, and chili peppers over low heat until softened, about 10 minutes.

Place the vegetables in a large serving bowl. Mix in the cooked rice, the peas, and jerk seasonings.

Serve warm.

Southern Fire-Roasted Fresh Ham

8-pound fresh ham, rind
    removed

Salt and pepper to taste

¼ cup packed brown sugar

½ teaspoon ground nutmeg

1 can beer

2 cloves garlic

Sprig fresh rosemary

Fresh ham is a pork leg that has not been salt- or sugar-cured or smoked—it's fresh. This, to some people, is the finest cut of pork available. It's very festive for holiday dining and really good eating any time of year!

Serves 10 to 12

Set your grill at 400 degrees. You will be cooking over indirect heat.

Trim the fat, leaving ¼ inch on the ham. Score it as you would a regular ham.

Salt and pepper the ham. Mix together the brown sugar and nutmeg. Spread it on the ham.

Place the beer, garlic, and rosemary in a roasting pan to make a basting liquid.

Roast the ham for 20 minutes at 400 degrees, then reduce heat to 325 degrees. Baste every 20 minutes. The ham is done when it reaches an internal temperature of 150 degrees. Let it rest for 20 minutes before carving. Serve with applesauce or sweet red pie cherries, thinned with a little red wine.

TAILGATE PARTY
Grilled Tenderloin of Pork with Grilled Green Apples and Mustard Sauce

Mustard sauce:

2 tablespoons olive oil

4 shallots, peeled and
    minced

2 cloves garlic, peeled and
    minced

2 tablespoons Wondra
    quick-blending flour

4 teaspoons Dijon-style
    mustard

1 cup chicken broth

½ cup heavy cream

¼ cup bourbon

Salt and pepper to taste

Tenderloin:

2 tenderloins, about 2
    pounds total; if less, buy
    an extra

3 tablespoons coarse-
    grained mustard

3 tablespoons all-purpose
    flour

4 tablespoons olive oil

Salt to taste

1 teaspoon cayenne pepper

2 to 3 sprigs fresh thyme

This is a succulent piece of meat; you'll need two pork fillets to serve six to eight people. Quantities, as always, depend on how many other mains and sides you are serving. Pork tenderloins are all meat, no fat or bone, no waste. Make the sauce in advance, and warm up when ready to serve the pork loins.

Serves 8

Heat the olive oil over a low flame. Stir in the shallots and garlic, and cook over low heat until softened.

Blend in the flour and stir until absorbed.

Whisk in the rest of the sauce ingredients, one at a time. When thick, pack up to take to your tailgate party. Just warm your sauce up at the last minute; don't get it too hot or it may curdle.

Rinse and pat the tenderloins dry.

In a small bowl, mix together the rest of the ingredients but the thyme to make a paste. Coat the tenderloins with the paste. Sprinkle with thyme and pack in aluminum foil until you arrive at your tailgate party.

Set the grill at 350 degrees. Grill the loins for

Grilled apples:

6 large Granny Smith apples, peeled, cored, and sliced horizontally, about ½ inch thick

6 teaspoons lemon juice

4 teaspoons brown sugar

Salt to taste

about 30 minutes; medium-rare is fine. Place on a platter and cover loosely with foil. Let the meat rest for 15 minutes before carving.

Cut the apples in rounds. Sprinkle on both sides with lemon juice. Sprinkle with the brown sugar and salt. Place in a plastic bag until you are ready to grill.

Place on the grill until sugar starts to caramelize. Serve with the pork.

BIG DADDY LOWDOWN

You've Got It Covered

Although it's best to serve steaks and other foods directly from the grill, sometimes circumstances require the chef to set aside already prepared items while other items cook. What's the best way to keep these items warm without drying them out?

Keep them covered and in a warm place, and always cook meat last.

Grilled Marinated Chicken Legs

6 chicken drumsticks and
6 thighs, rinsed and
patted dry

Marinade:

½ cup freshly squeezed
orange juice

Juice of ½ lemon

4 tablespoons orange
marmalade

½ cup dry white vermouth

1 teaspoon hot red pepper
sauce, or to taste

1 tablespoon soy sauce

½ teaspoon celery salt

1 teaspoon garlic powder

Chicken legs on the grill are lovely, but it's so easy to get into a rut. Try this marinade.

Serves 6 to 8

Mix all the marinade ingredients together. Place in a large plastic bag with the chicken. Marinate 4 to 6 hours.

Grill the chicken pieces over medium flame, at about 325 degrees, turning often, until browned, but not burned. You can baste with some additional white vermouth.

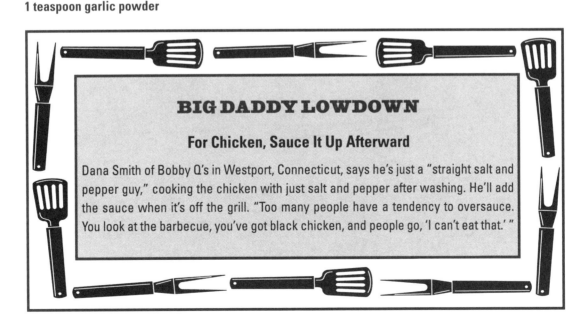

BIG DADDY LOWDOWN

For Chicken, Sauce It Up Afterward

Dana Smith of Bobby Q's in Westport, Connecticut, says he's just a "straight salt and pepper guy," cooking the chicken with just salt and pepper after washing. He'll add the sauce when it's off the grill. "Too many people have a tendency to oversauce. You look at the barbecue, you've got black chicken, and people go, 'I can't eat that.'"

Selection of Smoked Sausages with Various Breads and Mustards

Loaves of rye, sourdough,
and pumpernickel
A pot of hot sauerkraut
A pot of good baked beans
4 to 5 kinds of mustard
Pickle relish

This is a great way to do a tailgate! Either go to your local butcher shop or order sausages on the Web, where there is an infinite variety.

Just grill the sausages until well browned. Serve and let people help themselves to the condiments. If they are precooked, just heat them up!

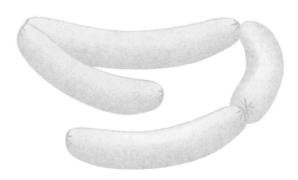

Clambake—On the Beach or in the Kitchen

1 large new galvanized-steel
    garbage can
Rocks from the shore
Plenty of wood and charcoal
2 pounds seaweed
1 quart bottled clam broth
10 chicken pieces (breasts,
    thighs, and drumsticks)
10 lobsters, claw bands
    removed
40 littleneck clams, well
    scrubbed, tightly closed
50 soft shelled clams, well
    scrubbed
20 ears of corn

On the side:
8 sticks unsalted butter,
    melted
8 lemons, cut in quarters

If you are going to do a clambake on the beach, be sure to get permission first from the owner or the Parks Department. Clambakes are a long and slow process. You can use the same ingredients for a smaller clambake in your kitchen.

Serves 10

You need to dig a hole in the sand, big enough to hold the can.

Line the hole with rocks, and then stack on wood and charcoal, and set afire.

Put seaweed on the bottom of the can and, when the fire has died down, place the can in the hole. The rocks will do the cooking.

Stack the ingredients in the order listed above. Cover the can.

Let the clambake cook for 2 hours.

Serve with plenty of melted butter and lots of lemons. Be sure to serve on an "elegant table-cloth"—once again, newspapers work just fine.

Baltimore Crab Cakes and Coleslaw

2 eggs, lightly beaten

1 cup soft bread crumbs

½ teaspoon prepared
   mustard

½ cup mayonnaise

Juice of ½ lemon

Salt and pepper to taste

½ teaspoon dried dill weed

1½ pounds Maryland lump
   crabmeat

1 cup fine cracker crumbs
   for coating

We have eaten crabs all over the East-ern Shore of Chesapeake Bay. Although you can get crabmeat that has been farmed in various exotic locations, Maryland blue crab is among the very best. And, it's the most expensive, but worth it. Some of the most interesting crab cakes we've enjoyed were ones made with minced country ham added. See page 168 for the coleslaw recipe.

Serves 6 to 8

Mix all the ingredients but crabmeat and cracker crumbs. Gently fold in the crabmeat and form into 8 patties.

Coat the patties with cracker crumbs. Fry in 340-degree peanut or canola oil until brown on both sides. Drain on paper towels. Serve the crab cakes with tartar sauce, lemon wedges, and coleslaw.

Maine Lobster Stew

To prepare the lobsters:

3 cups cold water

1 celery stalk, with leaves, chopped

1 carrot, peeled and chopped

4 peppercorns

1-inch-strip lemon peel

2 lobsters, about 1½ pounds each

Stew:

½ stick unsalted butter

3 tablespoons all-purpose flour

1 teaspoon celery salt

1 teaspoon Worcestershire sauce

Warm lobster stock and juices (must be warm for a smooth base)

1½ cups whole milk

1 cup heavy cream

Diced lobster with any coral (eggs) and green tamali (fat)

Salt and pepper to taste

¼ cup sherry (optional)

This is rich and satisfying. Serve with tiny oyster crackers. In New England, and even in New York City's famed Grand Central Oyster Bar, a stew is actually a creamy soup.

Serves 8

Bring the water to a boil in a large pot. Add the celery, carrot, peppercorns, and lemon peel. Remove claw bands from lobsters and carefully place in the pot. Cover and steam for 15 minutes.

Remove the lobsters and place them on a tray with a good rim; you'll want to reserve the juices that the lobsters release when you remove the meat.

Remove the meat and dice it. Strain the cooking stock and reserve it. Add the juice from the lobsters to the stock.

Melt the butter in a large pot and whisk in the flour, celery salt, and Worcestershire sauce. Cook, whisking over a low flame for 4 minutes. Slowly whisk in the warm stock and juices.

Add the milk, cream, and lobster. Heat over a low flame. Taste for seasonings and add the sherry, if desired.

Ladle into heated bowls.

Prince Edward Island Mussels— Billy Bi Soup

Mussels:

1 cup water

2 pounds well-scrubbed
   mussels (Make sure that
   the beards are removed
   and that they are tightly
   closed; discard any open
   or cracked mussels.)

1 shallot, chopped

1 clove garlic, cut up

¼ cup chopped parsley

½ cup dry white wine

Soup:

½ stick unsalted butter

4 tablespoons all-purpose
   flour

Reserved mussels and juice

2 cups heavy or whipping
   cream

1 cup milk

Salt and pepper to taste

This is a French and Canadian classic. Billy Bi has worked its way down both coastlines. It's sinfully delicious, with lots of cream and mussels!

Serves 6

Place all the mussel ingredients in a soup kettle. Bring to a boil. Have a large bowl handy. As soon as the mussels open, put them into the bowl.

Remove the mussels from the shells. Whirl them in the jar of your blender with the juices from the kettle. Reserve.

In a large soup kettle, melt the butter, whisk in the flour, and continue to whisk until the mixture is very smooth. Blend in the mussels and juice, then add the cream and milk.

Stir in salt and pepper to taste. This is a very thick soup.

Serve in warm bowls.

Prince Edward Island Mussels Grilled and Dressed with Special Sauce

6 to 8 pounds mussels, well
    scrubbed, beards
    removed, and tightly
    closed
1 cup white wine
1 cup water

Sauce:
1 cup of your favorite BBQ
    sauce
½ stick butter
1 tablespoon Worcestershire
    sauce
Juice of 1 lemon

This is a natural for mussel lovers. The sauce is a buttery combination of Worcestershire, BBQ, and, of course, lots of butter and lemon juice. You need a good loaf of French or Italian bread to sop up the juices. Figure on ½ to ⅔ pound of mussels per person, extra for big eaters.

Serves 12

Place the mussels on a metal tray or aluminum roasting pan on the grill. Pour the wine and water into the pan. When the mussels open, serve them with the sauce and plenty of French or Italian bread to sop up the juices.

Mix all the sauce ingredients in a pot and place over a low flame. Stir for about 5 minutes as butter melts. Remove after sauce reaches a low boil and pour over the mussels. Again, lots of toasted pieces of bread!

Sit outside and enjoy!

Chuck Wagon Chili and Biscuits

½ cup vegetable oil

4 pounds coarsely ground chuck or sirloin steak

1 tablespoon salt

Pepper to taste

2 tablespoons unsweetened cocoa powder

4 tablespoons chili powder, or to taste

1 tablespoon ground cumin, or to taste

½ teaspoon ground cinnamon

Hot red pepper sauce to taste

Freshly ground black pepper to taste

4 large onions, chopped

6 cloves garlic, chopped

½ cup bottled steak sauce

1 can rich beer (not light beer)

Two 28-ounce cans plum tomatoes

Four 14-ounce cans red kidney beans, drained, or two 1-pound bags red kidney beans, soaked overnight

The U.S. Cavalry subsisted on bison/buffalo meat. American ranchers generally hired ex-Army cooks to make their chuck wagon dinners. Today, there are huge cook-offs and contests for chili, and much pride is taken in getting a ribbon, a cup, or a check.

Makes 4 quarts

In a large soup kettle, heat the oil and brown the meat, mixing with a wooden spoon to break up clumps. Add the spices.

Sauté the onions and garlic. Add the rest of the ingredients to the same kettle and simmer for 4 hours over a good, hardwood fire. Stir frequently; burning or sticking is not a good thing.

Serve with biscuits, rice, or grits.

BIG DADDY LOWDOWN

Who Invented Chili?

There are passionate sides taken by the bean people and the no-bean people. And the controversy about the introduction of chili powder goes on and on. Was it a German lady living in Texas, or a Mexican lady? This one is delicious, but one of the greatest words of wisdom my daddy ever told me—no chili pleases everyone.

Buffalo Wings—The Real Thing!

4 sticks unsalted butter

½ cup of your favorite hot red pepper sauce, or to taste

¼ cup red wine vinegar

8 pounds chicken wings, tips cut off, joints cut to separate

Salt and pepper to taste

Most restaurants fry the wings in hot fat, then dip them in a mixture of butter, oil, and hot sauce.

Serves 14 to 20, depending on appetites

Set your grill or broiler on very high.

Melt the butter and stir in the hot sauce and vinegar. Brush on the wings.

Grill on one side, turning and grilling until just brown but not dried out.

Add salt and pepper at the end.

BIG DADDY LOWDOWN

Buffalo Wings from Buffalo, New York

The real Buffalo recipe came out of desperation. A woman who owned an Italian restaurant in Buffalo, New York, was closing up when her teenage son and a few of his friends arrived, hungry. She had a big bag of chicken wings, ready for making chicken soup in the morning. Instead, she reheated the pizza oven, poured melted butter, salt, and hot sauce on the wings, and flash-cooked them. The boys told their friends and the word spread!

German Potato Salad

4 slices bacon, fried crisp,
    drained on paper towels,
    and crumbled, fat
    reserved

½ cup cider vinegar

¾ cup olive oil

1 red onion, finely chopped

½ cup parsley, chopped

4 large Idaho or Yukon gold
    potatoes, peeled and cut
    in chunks

1 tablespoon salt for the
    potato water

Salt and pepper to taste

Celery salt to taste

Adding bacon to this is a nice touch, and serving the potato salad hot is very good indeed.

Serves 6 to 8

In a large salad bowl, mix the crumbled bacon, vinegar, olive oil, onion, parsley, and 1 teaspoon of the bacon drippings.

Boil the potatoes in enough salted water to cover until tender.

Drain the potatoes, and mix into the dressing while still hot. Taste for salt and pepper.

Sprinkle with celery salt.

Egg-and-Potato Salad

Dressing:

1 cup mayonnaise

¼ cup red wine vinegar

1 teaspoon prepared
   mustard, or to taste

4 large eggs, hard-boiled,
   peeled, and chopped

Salt and pepper to taste

Salad:

10 red bliss potatoes, cut in
   half and boiled in their
   skins until tender

2 stalks celery, chopped

1 red onion, chopped

Simple and very easy to make!

Serves 6

Mix all the dressing ingredients together in a large serving bowl.

Add the potatoes, celery, and onion to the dressing in the bowl. Mix to coat evenly and serve hot or chilled.

Broccoli, Cauliflower, and Potato Salad with Homemade Ranch Dressing

Dressing:

1 cup dairy sour cream

1 cup mayonnaise

2 teaspoons prepared
    mustard

1 tablespoon red or white
    wine vinegar

Juice of 1 lemon

1 teaspoon lemon zest

2 cloves garlic

1 soft-boiled egg

Salt and pepper to taste

Salad:

3 quarts water

1 tablespoon salt

1 head broccoli florets (no
    stems!), rinsed

1 head cauliflower, well
    trimmed, separated into
    florets, and rinsed

4 large Idaho potatoes,
    peeled and cut into
    chunks

This is such a healthy dish, you'll jump up and shout!

Serves 8

Whirl all the dressing ingredients in the jar of your blender. Pour into a large serving bowl.

Bring the water to a boil and add salt. Blanch the broccoli and cauliflower for 10 minutes. Remove from the water, shock in cold water, and drain.

Boil the potatoes until tender. Drain and cool.

Mix all the ingredients in the serving bowl, coating everything nicely.

Cucumber Salad with Watercress

Dressing:

1 cup olive oil

Juice of ½ lemon

1 tablespoon cider vinegar

½ teaspoon celery salt

½ teaspoon caraway seed

½ teaspoon white sugar

½ teaspoon hot paprika

Salt and pepper to taste

Salad:

2 bunches watercress or
arugula

1 head Bibb or Boston
lettuce, washed

3 cucumbers (the long,
skinny English ones are
thin-skinned and best in
salad)

This has a slightly Norse flair to it, and goes well with any fish. It's particularly wonderful with salmon.

Serves 6 to 8

Mix all the dressing ingredients together and set aside.

Wash all of the lettuces, remove stems, and dry in a spinner or on paper towels. Arrange the lettuces on a platter.

Slice the cucumbers thinly over the platter of lettuce (it's your choice whether to peel the cucumbers). Chill, drizzle with dressing, and serve.

Tomato and Red-Onion Salad
with Greek Olives and Goat Cheese

Dressing:

¾ cup extra-virgin olive oil

3 tablespoons red wine
   vinegar

Salt and pepper to taste

Salad:

4 cups of your favorite
   lettuce, washed, dried,
   and torn in small pieces

4 pounds red ripe or
   heirloom tomatoes, cores
   trimmed, sliced

1 red onion, thinly sliced

¼ cup fresh mint leaves,
   shredded

1 teaspoon dried oregano
   leaves

30 Greek olives, such as
   kalamata

6 ounces goat cheese

This is best made when you have lots of red, ripe tomatoes in your garden or can get them from a farm stand. The simpler the dressing for this, the better!

Serves 8

Mix all the dressing ingredients in a bottle and shake well.

Arrange the greens on a platter. Slowly stack up the tomatoes and red onion. Sprinkle with mint and oregano. Decoratively place the olives around the platter.

Chill the cheese and slice it with dental floss (non-minted). Arrange it over the tomatoes.

Drizzle with the dressing and serve.

Corn Bread

4 slices bacon

1½ cups all-purpose flour

¾ cup yellow or white
cornmeal

¼ cup packed dark brown
sugar

2 teaspoons baking powder

1 cup buttermilk

½ stick butter, melted, plus 1
teaspoon bacon fat

2 whole eggs

½ cup grated, sharp cheddar
cheese, optional

Corn bread does not have to be bland and blah. It can be really delicious with the addition of some bacon and bacon fat. Also, using brown sugar or molasses, instead of white sugar, makes a big difference in flavor. Bits of cheese can also be added for extra nutrition.

Makes sixteen 2-inch squares

Set your oven at 400 degrees. Prepare an 8x8-inch baking pan with nonstick spray.

Fry the bacon, drain on paper towels, and crumble. Reserve fat.

Mix all of the dry ingredients in a bowl. Whisk in the milk, butter, and eggs and then stir in the cheddar cheese, if desired.

Pour into the prepared baking pan. Bake for 25 to 30 minutes.

The Best Coleslaw

Dressing:

2 cups mayonnaise

½ cup cider vinegar

1 tablespoon white sugar

1 tablespoon dry mustard

1 teaspoon chili powder

½ cup chili sauce

1 teaspoon celery salt

1 teaspoon celery seed

Freshly ground black pepper
  to taste (start with ½
  teaspoon)

2 teaspoons caraway seed,
  optional

Slaw:

5-pound head of green
  cabbage, outer leaves
  and core removed

5 large carrots, peeled

1 very sweet white onion,
  such as Vidalia; you may
  want to use 2, according
  to taste

There are hundreds of recipes for coleslaw out there. We like this one best.

Serves 12 to 14, depending on the size of the cabbage and whatever else you are serving

Mix the dressing ingredients together and refrigerate.

You can shred the cabbage and carrot in your food processor. Or, using a sharp knife, slice thin. Place in a large bowl.

Peel and slice the onion paper-thin.

Mix the dressing with the cabbage, carrot, and onion. Chill and serve.

Old-Fashioned Drop Biscuits

2 cups all-purpose flour

1 tablespoon white sugar, or
   to taste

1 teaspoon salt

4 teaspoons baking powder

½ cup heavy or whipping
   cream

We always liked these better than the neatly rolled-out circles. With their little peaks sticking up, they make a far more interesting biscuit. They can also be used for a really country shortcake.

Makes 16 biscuits

Set your oven at 425 degrees. Prepare a cookie sheet with nonstick spray.

Mix all the ingredients in a bowl just until combined. Do not overbeat.

Drop the biscuits with a tablespoon onto the prepared cookie sheet.

Bake for 15 minutes.

Note: For extra-rich biscuits, you can add 4 tablespoons butter to the dough.

Grill-Roasted Sourdough Bread with Garlic and Jack Cheese

1 loaf Italian sourdough
    bread
½ stick butter
¼ cup olive oil
3 cloves garlic, mashed
½ teaspoon salt
3 ounces Monterey Jack or
    pepper Jack cheese,
    grated, or 6 tablespoons
    grated Parmesan cheese

Serves 6 to 8

Score the bread down the middle lengthwise. Score the loaf crosswise. Melt the butter and add the olive oil, garlic, and salt. Spread the sections apart and paint with butter mixture.

Grill the bread until lightly browned. Sprinkle on the cheese and continue to grill until the cheese melts.

Chapter 9

Exotic International Recipes

hat do people on an island in the Pacific Ocean have in common with a family in New England? You guessed it: open-fire cooking. People have been cooking with open fire since man discovered how to rub two sticks together.

Here are some fun and delicious recipes that are popular around the world. With them, we've tried to capture a little of the adventure and the excitement of every continent, whether it be the elegance and opulent sophistication of Northern Italy, the casual party fun of a real Hawaiian luau, or a Cajun gumbo feast.

LUAU

The original Hawaiian feast began serving Westerners in the 1800s. Most luaus feature a roast suckling pig. The lush fruits, the fish from the sea, and the warmth of the people and the sun make luau a great success, gastronomically and commercially.

BIG DADDY LOWDOWN

A Word About Poi

Unless you are a poi aficionado, you probably won't like it. Poi is made of ground taro root, which is dark gray and very gooey, and although Islanders love it, this food is an acquired taste.

Grilled Hawaiian Tuna Steaks
with Citrus Beurre Blanc

Sauce:

4 shallots, minced

2 tablespoons lemon juice

2 tablespoons orange-juice
concentrate

¼ cup chicken or fish stock

2 sticks unsalted butter

Salt and pepper to taste

Fish:

8 tuna steaks

4 teaspoons olive oil

Salt and pepper to taste

¾ cup chopped macadamia
nuts, for garnish

Hawaiian tuna is considered by many to be the best on the planet, and while this sauce is not Hawaiian, it's out of this world!

Serves 8

Place the shallots in a mixture of the lemon juice and orange-juice concentrate. Whisk in the fish stock.

Slowly whisk in bits of the cold butter, whisking vigorously after each addition until the sauce is very smooth. Add salt and pepper to taste. Set aside.

Start a good fire, waiting until the flame subsides, or set your grill at 400 degrees.

Rub the tuna steaks with the olive oil and sprinkle with salt and pepper. Grill 4 minutes per side. Place on a platter and spoon on the reserved sauce. Sprinkle with chopped macadamia nuts.

Grilled Mahimahi

Sauce:

½ cup soy sauce

Juice of 1 lime

1 clove garlic, minced

1 teaspoon Chinese mustard

1 tablespoon peeled and
    minced fresh gingerroot

8 mahimahi steaks

This is a firm, white fish, native to tropical waters and common in Hawaii. It has become popular in the United States for its delicate flavor. The word "mahimahi" means "strong-strong" in Hawaiian, and the fish can grow to 50 pounds!

Serves 8

Mix all the sauce ingredients together. Set aside.

Set your grill on medium-high.

Paint the reserved sauce on the fish and grill on each side for about 4 minutes, depending on thickness. Turn once.

Side of Fried Coconut Chips

1 coconut, halved, milk
    saved for another purpose
1 inch hot canola or peanut
    oil in a frying pan
Salt and pepper to taste

The serving size depends on the size of the coconut.

Cut the coconut into thin chips.

Heat the oil to 350 degrees. Fry chips until golden. Drain on paper towels, and sprinkle with salt and pepper.

Grilled Bananas

4 large bananas, on the
    green side, peeled and
    split
4 teaspoons butter, melted
Salt and pepper to taste or, if
    as dessert, brown sugar

These are very good as a side dish or a dessert, grilled with brown sugar.

Serves 4 to 6

Brush the bananas with the melted butter and place on the grill for about 2 minutes per side.

If you are serving them for dessert, be sure to sprinkle on the sugar just before cooking.

Serve with coconut ice cream, or honey and chopped nuts.

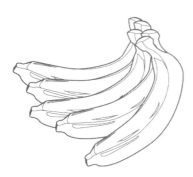

CAJUN GUMBO FEAST

Filé, the dried and then ground leaves of the sassafras tree or bush, was first used as seasoning by the Choctaw tribes of Louisiana. The invading Europeans, Spanish, and French settlers liked it so much that they adopted it into their cooking. Many gumbo recipes are designed to serve between 25 and 100 people. Now that's one very big pot of stew! This is a tasty recipe and you certainly can multiply it to serve more. Serve with grilled bread (see page 170). All gumbo is based on roux, which both flavors and thickens the stew.

Roux:

2 tablespoons all-purpose flour

2 tablespoons fat or vegetable oil

Gumbo:

2 quarts rich chicken broth

½ stick butter

2 quarts tomatoes, crushed (fresh or canned)

1 quart sliced okra

2 bell peppers, cored, seeded, and chopped

1 quart celery, chopped, with tops

1 quart onions, chopped

10 cloves garlic, crushed

2 tablespoons Cajun blackening spice (see recipe on page 178)

2 tablespoons Old Bay seasoning

2 tablespoons red pepper sauce, or to taste

2 tablespoons commercial shrimp or crab boiling spice

5 to 6 pounds fresh shrimp, peeled, deveined, and chopped

Salt and black pepper to taste

Gumbo

Serves 20

To prepare roux, blend the flour and oil in a heavy frying pan. Cook, stirring, until the mixture just starts to brown. Remove from the heat and let it finish cooking until brown. Set aside.

To make the gumbo, heat the broth in a large stockpot. Add the butter and let it melt.

Add the rest of the ingredients but the shrimp, stirring after each addition.

Cover and let simmer for 3 hours.

Mix some of the liquid from the stew into the reserved roux. Stir the roux mixture back into the pot.

Add the shrimp and simmer for another 2 hours.

Taste for salt and extra pepper.

Blackened Catfish

Blackening spice:
¼ cup freshly ground black
   pepper

¼ cup kosher salt

5 tablespoons sweet paprika

2 tablespoons lemon zest

2 tablespoons cayenne
   pepper

1 tablespoon dried thyme
   leaves

1 tablespoon garlic powder

Catfish:
8 fresh catfish fillets, about 6
   ounces each, rinsed and
   patted dry

Just about any fish can be blackened with special spices. And there are as many recipes for blackening seasonings as there are Cajun cooks. We have developed this one. Of course, it makes a delicious crust on the fish, and can be used either on the grill or in a big, black, cast-iron frying pan. Make a lot of the spice and save some for the next time.

Serves 8

Mix all the seasoning ingredients well and store in a tightly closed jar in the refrigerator.

Sprinkle the fillets with the spices, cover, and let rest for 1 hour. Press the spices into the fish with the back of a spoon.

Set your grill on high, or use a good hot charcoal fire.

Grill the fish for about 2 to 3 minutes per side.

Serve with rice and vegetables.

Corn Soufflé

½ stick butter

½ cup minced onion

2 tablespoons all-purpose
flour

¾ cup warm milk or half-and-
half

Two 10-ounce boxes frozen
corn, thawed

Two 10-ounce boxes frozen
creamed corn, or two 12-
ounce cans creamed corn

¼ teaspoon ground nutmeg

½ bunch chives, minced

1 teaspoon hot red pepper
sauce

Salt and freshly ground
pepper to taste

6 extra-large eggs,
separated

½ cup roasted red peppers,
chopped, optional

2 pickled jalapeño peppers,
chopped, optional

½ cup fresh bread crumbs,
for topping

There is no reason not to use either canned or frozen creamed corn for this unless you have a garden full of very young, beautiful corn.

Serves 8

Set your oven at 400 degrees.

Prepare a 3-quart soufflé dish with nonstick spray.

Melt the butter and sauté the onion until soft. Blend in the flour and cook until smooth, about 3 minutes. Whisk in the warm milk or half-and-half.

Add the corn, nutmeg, chives, hot pepper sauce, and salt and pepper. Mix well.

Separate the eggs and beat the yolks until pale yellow and light. Add to the corn mixture. Beat the whites until stiff peaks form.

Fold the egg whites into the corn mixture. Add the optional items, if desired.

Pour into the prepared soufflé dish. Sprinkle with the bread crumbs. Bake at 400 degrees for 20 minutes, reduce heat to 350 degrees, and bake for another 30 minutes.

Classic Spanish Paella

2 chickens, cut into 8 pieces
each

¾ cup seasoned flour (add
salt, pepper, and paprika)

⅔ cup olive oil

1 pound chorizo, a Spanish
sausage that is widely
available, cut in chunks

1 cup chopped sweet onion

4 cloves garlic, chopped

3 cups uncooked short-
grained rice

13-ounce can crushed
tomatoes

½ teaspoon saffron threads

Plenty of freshly ground
black pepper

2 cups clam broth

2 cups chicken broth

6 cups water

24 littleneck clams, scrubbed
and tightly closed

24 mussels, beards removed,
scrubbed and tightly
closed

1 bunch parsley, rinsed and
chopped

1 pound bay scallops

2 pounds raw shrimp, peeled
and deveined

There are as many recipes for paella as there are home cooks and chefs who prepare it. The kinds of seafood included in the recipe are simply whatever happens to be available. If you do not have a large enamel-coated, metal paella pan, it will be hard to get the rice evenly cooked. You might try using a large roasting pan; however, if you really love paella, it's worth it to buy a proper pan. The most common mistake when preparing paella is to put all of the seafood in at once; instead, you should add the elements in the order in which they cook, and since the shrimp and scallops take the least time, they go in last.

Serves 14 to 18

Dip the chicken in the seasoned flour. Brown it in olive oil in a paella dish or large skillet. Remove to paper towels to drain. Brown the chorizo in the same oil, then remove and drain.

Sauté the onion and garlic for 4 to 5 minutes, until softened.

Add the rice and stir to coat, then add the tomatoes, saffron, and pepper. Add the liquids.

Return the chicken and chorizo to the pan.

Cover with aluminum foil and let simmer for 15 minutes, either on top of the stove or in the oven (oven set at 350 degrees).

Stir the rice and add the clams and continue to simmer for another 10 minutes.

Put the mussels in, poking them down into the rice, and simmer for another 10 minutes.

When the clams and mussels are just starting to open, sprinkle with parsley and add the rest of the seafood. Cook for 2 to 3 minutes, until shrimp turns pink.

> *Note:* **It's nice to have a toasty crust of rice on the bottom of the pan. Some people think that's the best part.**

ITALIAN FEAST

A proper Italian meal will include a pasta course, a fish course, a meat course with vegetables, a salad course, and a dessert, with an appropriate wine to go with each.

Mediterranean Bronzini

Sauce:

1 tablespoon butter

2 cloves garlic, mashed

½ cup olive oil

1 teaspoon kosher salt

1 teaspoon red pepper flakes

2 tablespoons orange juice

1 teaspoon orange zest

1 tablespoon lemon juice

¼ cup parsley, finely minced

Fish:

8 bronzini fillets, 6 ounces
   each

4 teaspoons tiny capers, for
   garnish

The United States is beginning to get bronzini, flown in from the Mediterranean. It's a fine, white fish with a mild texture that lends itself to tomato or citrus saucing. We recommend a classically simple sauce. You will want to brush some on the fish prior to grilling, then drizzle the rest on top when you serve it.

Serves 8

Melt the butter and add the garlic. Sauté gently.

Add the rest of the ingredients. Set aside for use on fish and for final dressing sauce.

Set your grill on high, about 400 degrees.

Spread the fillets on a grilling rack and spoon half the sauce over the fish.

Grill for about 4 minutes. Drizzle with more sauce, and garnish with capers.

Northern Italian Grilled Veal Tenderloin

2 veal tenderloins, any blue film trimmed off

Sprinkling of Wondra quick-blending flour

Salt and freshly ground pepper

2 tablespoons Dijon-style mustard

3 tablespoons lemon juice

3 tablespoons unsalted butter, at room temperature

Sauce:

¼ cup dry white wine

½ cup chicken broth

2 tablespoons butter

Juice of 1 lemon

This recipe was contributed by Chef Patricio Merino, of Tenero in South Norwalk, Connecticut. He points out that the butt end of the tenderloin is better for sautéing or grilling than the other end, which is very thin. Of course, it can be used in a sauté. Each loin weighs about 12 ounces and serves 3 to 4. Polenta and broccoli rabe go well with this.

Serves 6 to 8

Set your grill at 400 degrees, or coals to very hot.

Sprinkle the veal with flour, salt and pepper.

Make a paste of the mustard, lemon juice, and butter. Rub it all over the tenderloins.

Grill the veal for about 3 to 4 minutes per side. Let rest on a warm platter, covered, while making the sauce.

Reduce the wine and broth in a saucepan. Swirl in the butter and lemon juice. Add any juices from the veal.

Slice the veal in ⅓-inch rounds and serve with the sauce.

Sicilian Stuffed Squid

Stuffing:

1 tablespoon butter

3 tablespoons olive oil

2 cloves garlic, minced

6 scallions, trimmed and
 minced

1 teaspoon dried oregano
 leaves

½ pound raw shrimp, peeled,
 deveined, and chopped

Juice of ½ lemon

Salt and lots of freshly
 ground black pepper or to
 taste

To assemble the dish:

12 ounces of your favorite
 tomato sauce (marinara,
 meatless)

Twelve 3- to 4-inch calamari
 tubes (squid), cleaned
 and peeled

Stuffing, above

You will need small- to medium-size squid tubes for this. They must be cleaned. You can use the tentacles in the stuffing, but I prefer to deep-fry them to go on the side. We love using shrimp in the stuffing. Your quantities will vary according to the size differences in the squid.

Serves 6 as an appetizer

Melt the butter in a sauté pan, and add the olive oil, garlic, and scallions. Sauté for 6 minutes. Remove from the heat.

Add the rest of the stuffing ingredients and mix well. Set aside.

Set your oven at 300 degrees or the grill on indirect heat.

Using a large, flat baking dish or gratin pan, spread the bottom with a film of sauce.

Stuff the squid and arrange them in the pan. Cover with the remaining sauce. Cover with aluminum foil. Bake about 20 minutes, until the squid just begins to bubble. Do not overcook! If you do, the squid will get tough!

Tricolored Rotini Pasta with Asparagus Tips, Country Ham, and Monterey Jack Cheese

1 pound asparagus, tips
removed, stalks reserved
for another use
1 pound tricolored rotini
½ cup olive oil
4 cloves garlic, peeled and
chopped
1 cup finely chopped country
ham
1 cup shredded Monterey
Jack cheese
Plenty of freshly ground
black pepper, skip the
salt, as the ham is salty
½ bunch parsley, rinsed,
dried, and chopped, for
garnish
Parmesan cheese to taste

This is so Italian-American. We love the thin, young asparagus for this. Use only the tips; the stalks go into soup. Monterey Jack cheese has a fine flavor and melts well.

Serves 4

Blanch the asparagus tips in boiling, salted water for 3 minutes. Drop into ice water to shock and save color. Start the water for the rotini, add salt, and then add the pasta after the water comes to a boil.

Heat the olive oil in a large pan and add the garlic.

Sauté for 5 minutes while cooking the pasta. Drain the pasta when cooked.

Add the ham and asparagus tips to the garlic and oil. Mix in the hot pasta and the cheese. Mix well.

Garnish with the parsley and Parmesan and serve in warm bowls.

Roasted Garlic with Melted Fontina Cheese on Toasted Bread with Olives

2 heads garlic

6 tablespoons olive oil

1 loaf Italian or French bread

1 cup shredded Fontina
cheese

Assortment of Italian or
Spanish olives

Roasted garlic is excellent in soups, stews, and salad dressings. The garlic becomes sweet and mild when roasted, losing any pungency.

Serves 6 as antipasto

Slice the tips off the garlic, slicing crosswise about ¼ inch from the top. Leave the root ends intact.

Place the garlic heads on pieces of aluminum foil. Sprinkle each of the garlic heads with 1 teaspoon of the olive oil. Make packets of the foil and bake in a 350-degree oven for 1 hour.

Slice the bread. Place on a cookie sheet and toast one side. When the garlic is done and cool enough to handle, squeeze the garlic out clove by clove into the remaining olive oil.

Mash the garlic and oil together and spread on the untoasted side of the bread. Sprinkle with the Fontina cheese. Toast in the oven until the cheese melts. Serve with olives on the side.

Chapter 10

Something Different: Why Didn't I Think of That?

There's everyday grilling and then there's truly creative cooking. We want you to be versatile and imaginative as you approach your holiday feasts. One of the great things about outdoor grilling is that there really are no rules—except maybe that anything goes. You can improvise as needed, depending on what ingredients are in the house and what you are inclined to enjoy.

Suppose your Uncle Butch calls up and tells you he's got some fresh-killed deer—why not enjoy some Venison Burgers with Raisin Relish? Or, you've got some leftover turkey from Thanksgiving—how about bringing some international flavorings and creating Grilled Curried Turkey Burgers with Chutney?

You don't have to be a wizard to pull magic out of your chef's hat. This chapter shows some new ways to look at what otherwise might be everyday meals.

Venison Burgers with Raisin Relish

Relish:
½ cup white raisins

½ cup apricot nectar

1 tablespoon chili sauce

Juice of ½ lemon

1 teaspoon curry powder

½ teaspoon hot red pepper
  sauce, or to taste

Salt and pepper to taste

Burgers:
1½ pounds ground venison

1 teaspoon salt

Pepper to taste

1 tablespoon bottled steak
  sauce

8 strips bacon

4 favorite burger rolls

You can buy ground venison, venison steaks, roasts, and chops on the Web. Grilled venison burgers are delicious.

Serves 4

Mix together the raisins and nectar in a small saucepan. Bring to a boil.

Remove from the heat and let stand until the raisins are plump.

Stir in the rest of the ingredients.

Taste for salt and pepper and set aside.

Set your grill at about 400 degrees, or prepare coals until white-hot. Adding some mesquite chips will be an excellent touch.

Mix the venison with the salt, pepper, and steak sauce in a large bowl.

Form 4 patties. Place 4 strips of bacon on the grill. Put a patty on top of each. Place another strip of bacon on top of each patty. Because the venison is very lean, you need this to prevent the burgers from drying out.

Serve rare with the reserved relish.

Grilled Eggplant with Melted Cheese for Hot Sandwiches

4 small, skinny eggplants, cut in ⅓-inch slices

¼ cup of your favorite vinaigrette

4 rolls

4 slices white American cheese

½ cup commercial tomato sauce, warmed

Grilled eggplant, juicy and succulent, makes a terrific sandwich, dressed with some cheese and a little tomato sauce. If you use hero sandwich rolls, split and toasted, it's very delicious.

Makes 4 sandwiches

Prepare a grilling grid with nonstick spray.

Brush both sides of the eggplant slices with vinaigrette.

Grill the eggplant for 3 minutes per side. Toast the rolls. Arrange the eggplant on the rolls. Add the cheese and, using indirect heat, toast the cheese. Serve with warm tomato sauce on the side.

Grilled Portobello Mushrooms for Sandwiches with Roast Red Pepper/Cheese Sauce

Pepper/cheese sauce:

1 cup crumbled Gorgonzola
   cheese

½ cup mayonnaise

2 tablespoons chopped
   roasted red pepper, from a
   jar is fine

¼ cup of your favorite
   vinaigrette

Mushrooms:

4 portobello mushrooms,
   about 4 inches across,
   stems removed, cleaned
   by brushing off

¼ cup balsamic vinaigrette

Salt and pepper to taste

4 good-sized burger rolls

Serves 4

Mix all the sauce ingredients together in a small saucepan. Set aside.

Brush the mushrooms with the vinaigrette. Grill over high heat until mushrooms are good and hot and starting to sizzle.

Warm the sauce until the cheese melts. Slice the mushrooms thinly, like you would for a roast beef sandwich. Stack on the rolls, dress with cheese sauce, and slurp away!

Grilled Curried Turkey Burgers with Chutney

1¼ pounds ground turkey meat (try to get the dark, it's tastier)

1 tablespoon curry powder, or to taste

¼ cup plain nonfat yogurt

2 tablespoons bottled steak sauce, or to taste

Salt and pepper to taste

These make a nice main course over rice with the chutney on the side. Major Grey's makes a very tasty chutney.

Serves 4

Set your grill on medium, about 350 degrees, or let the coals die down.

While the grill is heating, mix all of the ingredients in a large bowl until well blended.

Form turkey into 4 generous patties. Grill about 6 minutes per side, until well done.

Season with salt and pepper to taste.

Serve with rice and chutney. Peanuts make a nice garnish.

Grilled Ham Steaks with Peaches

¼ cup packed brown sugar

¼ cup prepared mustard

½ teaspoon ground cloves

¼ teaspoon ground cinnamon

½ teaspoon ground
   cardamom

¼ cup orange juice

1 tablespoon orange zest

1-inch-thick ham steak,
   about 1½ pounds

4 large, firm, ripe peaches,
   halved, pits removed

This is a no-brainer. Get a nice thick piece of precooked ham, make the coating, and grill along with the peaches.

Serves 4

Set your grill on high. Mix together the sugar, mustard, cloves, cinnamon, cardamom, orange juice, and zest. Spread it on the ham steaks and the peaches.

Grill the ham until the sugar starts to caramelize. Turn the ham.

Grill the peaches when you turn the ham.

BIG DADDY LOWDOWN

The Tong Dynasty

Always use tongs or a spatula—never a fork—to turn over a steak during grilling. Also, resist the temptation to use a fork to test the steak for doneness while it's being grilled. A fork will pierce the meat and allow the juices to seep out.

Grilled Lamb Steak
with Curry Mustard Sauce

Four 6-ounce lamb steaks, or
    two 12-ounce lamb
    steaks
Salt and pepper to taste
Juice of 1 lemon

Sauce:
1 cup plain low-fat yogurt
¼ cup minced scallions
1 tablespoon curry powder
1 teaspoon dry English
    mustard
Juice of ½ lime
2 tablespoons chopped fresh
    mint leaves
Salt and pepper to taste

The best lamb steaks are cut from the leg. They often need to be tenderized with lemon juice.

Serves 4

Lay the steaks on a piece of waxed paper and sprinkle on both sides with salt, pepper, and lemon juice.

Let stand for 20 minutes, or refrigerate.

Set your grill on medium-high, about 375 degrees.

Mix all the sauce ingredients together in a bowl and set aside.

Grill the steaks for about 5 minutes per side.

Serve the lamb with the yogurt mixture on the side or as a dipping sauce.

Loin Lamb Chops with Garlic and Lemon

4 thick loin lamb chops

Salt and cayenne pepper to taste

4 cloves garlic, slivered

4 strips lemon peel

Juice of 1 lemon

We like these to be at least 1 inch thick. Trim off the fat, as lamb fat is strong and difficult to digest.

Serves 4

Set your grill at 350 degrees, and plan to use indirect heat.

Sprinkle the chops with salt and cayenne pepper. Poke the slivers of garlic into the chops, going between the bones and the meat. Using toothpicks, skewer the lemon peel to the meat. Sprinkle the chops with lemon juice.

Grill about 8 minutes per side, until pink and moist inside.

Serve with grilled tomatoes, if desired.

Country-Style BBQ Pork Ribs with Old-Fashioned Sauce

8 pounds country-style pork
spareribs, cut into 2-rib
portions (Because of the
bones, you need a lot of
weight to get a little
meat.)

1 cup vinegar

2 quarts fresh water, or to
cover

4 cloves garlic, do not peel

2 onions, cut in half

4 coriander seeds, bruised
with a mortar and pestle

4 whole cloves, bruised in a
mortar and pestle

6 whole black peppercorns,
bruised

1 whole lemon, cut in
quarters

1 tablespoon kosher salt

These big, fat ribs are cooked twice for tenderness.

Serves 4

Place the ribs in a pot with vinegar, water to cover, and the rest of the ingredients. Simmer for 4 hours.

Set your grill on low with plenty of good mesquite chips that you've soaked in advance.

Drain the ribs. Place them on the grill and cook for another hour, or more.

Serve with your favorite BBQ sauce on the side.

BIG DADDY LOWDOWN

Saucy Susan

When items come off the grill, the amount of sauce you'll want to serve alongside depends on how potent the condiment is. Texture counts too: a thick sauce or salsa gives more mileage than a less concentrated one.

Grilled French Toast Sandwiches Filled with Brie and Prosciutto (or Country) Ham

6 eggs

½ cup milk

8 thick slices good bread

4 ounces Brie, cut in thin slices, right out of the refrigerator (If it's not cold, you won't be able to cut it.)

4 thin slices prosciutto or country ham

The best French toast is made with a Jewish bread called challah. Cut thick, it sops up the eggs and milk. However, prosciutto or country ham adds a special touch with the richness of the Brie. Serve for lunch, brunch, or supper.

Serves 4

Whisk together the eggs and milk in a large, flat bowl. Soak the bread until it has absorbed all the liquid.

Set your grill on medium, about 300 degrees, or wait until the coals die down.

Place all of the bread on the grill and toast until nicely brown. Turn and place the Brie and the ham on 4 of the grilled sides. Close the sandwiches and toast on both sides.

Cut the sandwiches in pieces and serve with maple syrup or with mustard.

Grilled Polenta Patties

6½ cups water, or half
chicken broth and half
water, or half water and
half milk
1 tablespoon salt
2 cups yellow cornmeal
Optional: ½ cup grated
Parmesan cheese; 1
bunch scallions, rinsed
and minced; chopped
onions and garlic;
sautéed herbs, dry or
fresh, to taste

Polenta is a fancy way of saying con-
gealed cornmeal. You can cook the cornmeal with water, broth, or milk. You can add
all sorts of delicious cheeses, herbs, and vegetables to it, too. Always make a lot, it's fine
in the fridge for several days, or you can
freeze it! Grilled is delicious. Try this as a
terrific side, with meat or chicken and gravy.

Serves 8

Prepare a 9x13-inch glass baking dish with
nonstick spray.

Bring the water, broth, or milk mixture to a
boil. Add salt. In a slow stream add the cornmeal,
stirring constantly.

Cook, stirring, for 20 minutes. When done, you
may add ½ cup Parmesan cheese, or scallions, or
onions and garlic, or herbs.

Pour the polenta into the prepared dish.

Chill the polenta for 2 to 3 hours. When ready
to grill, cut into squares and grill. Serve with gravy
or butter.

Grilled Stuffed Green Tomatoes

8 medium or 4 huge green
tomatoes, cut in half
crosswise

4 teaspoons cooked polenta

4 tablespoons crumbled goat
cheese

½ bunch chives, chopped

½ stick butter or margarine

You need to find the largest tomatoes available—like big, green beefsteaks. Provide one half huge tomato per person, or 1 whole medium tomato.

Serves 8

Do this over indirect heat while you are grilling a main course.

Scoop the seeds out of the tomato halves with a melon-ball spoon.

Mix together the polenta, goat cheese, and chives. Work into the cut tomato halves. Dot with the butter.

Place on pieces of aluminum foil or in an aluminum pan. Grill over indirect heat until hot and delicious.

BIG DADDY LOWDOWN

"Side"-bar

Maple wood side cutting boards, built into some grilling stations, make food preparation even easier. You'll appreciate their convenience and time-saving value when you want to cook, heat, or sauté side dishes.

Fried Green Tomatoes

4 very large green tomatoes,
   rinsed and cut into thick
   (about ½-inch) slices,
   core ends removed

Salt and pepper

1 cup buttermilk whisked
   with 1 whole egg

Mixture of 1 cup cornmeal
   and 1 cup corn flour

½ inch peanut or canola oil
   (the old recipes call for
   lard)

These should have a real crunch on the outside and be piquant on the inside! The number of servings depends on the size of your tomatoes. A dozen small or medium tomatoes will serve 6 to 8 people. Larger tomatoes will serve more.

Serves 8

Sprinkle the tomatoes with salt and pepper.

Dip the salted tomatoes in the buttermilk mixture.

Mix the cornmeal and corn flour on a large piece of waxed paper. Coat the tomato slices with the mixture.

Heat the oil to 375 degrees. Fry the tomatoes until crisp and crunchy.

Drain and serve.

Baked Stuffed Tomatoes

36 cherry tomatoes

1 cup crabmeat, chopped
finely

1 stick margarine or butter,
at room temperature

4 tablespoons minced
parsley

1 teaspoon dried oregano
leaves

½ teaspoon hot red pepper
sauce

1 teaspoon paprika

⅔ cup fine bread crumbs

This side is the most fun when you use cherry tomatoes, especially yellow ones. Yellow tomatoes of any size are sweeter than red ones.

Serves 12 as hors d'oeuvres

Either set the oven at 400 degrees or your grill on high, over indirect heat.

Slice the stem ends off the tomatoes and scoop out the centers with a melon-ball spoon. Place the tomatoes in a shallow aluminum baking pan.

Mix the rest of the ingredients, except the bread crumbs, together. Using a teaspoon, stuff the tomatoes.

Sprinkle with the bread crumbs.

Bake for 15 minutes, or until hot and brown.

World-Class Mashed Potatoes

4 large Idaho potatoes,
   peeled and cut in large
   chunks
1 tablespoon salt
½ stick butter
Salt, pepper, and ground
   nutmeg to taste
1 cup whole milk or half-
   and-half

You can add roasted garlic to mashed potatoes, or sautéed onions, or anchovy paste. Whatever you do, if the basic mashed potato isn't terrific, you'll end up with nada. So, start with the basic and go from there.

Serves 8

Boil the potatoes in enough salted water to cover until tender. Then put them through a ricer or in a bowl and use your electric mixer, only on low. If you run the mixer on high, the starch will excite and turn the potatoes to library paste.

With your mixer running on low, or adding to riced potatoes, stir in butter, making sure that it melts. Add salt, pepper, and nutmeg.

Slowly add the milk or half-and-half. When you get to the desired consistency, add no more milk. If the potatoes are still too stiff, use some of the water you have boiled them in to give the mash a nice, light consistency.

Keep warm in the oven, covered, on low (200 degrees) until ready to serve. When done, fold in herbs and sautéed onions, if desired.

Carrot Slaw

1 cup black or white raisins

6 large carrots, peeled

1 sweet white onion, such as Vidalia

1 jicama, peeled

2 medium zucchini

Juice of 1 lemon

3 celery stalks, chopped

Coleslaw dressing (see page 168)

This recipe makes healthy eating fun! Use the dressing from the coleslaw recipe on page 168. This recipe is great for the kids!

Serves 8 to 10

Soak the raisins in 1 cup hot water. Using your food processor, grate the carrots, onion, jicama, and zucchini. Sprinkle with lemon juice, tossing to cover. Add the chopped celery.

Mix in the dressing. Cover and refrigerate.

BIG DADDY LOWDOWN

Early Bird Special

Why not whip up some side dishes the night before? Many sides will keep for several days if properly refrigerated.

Macaroni Salad

Dressing:

2 raw eggs (pasteurized, if
 you have concerns)

½ inch anchovy paste

2 cloves garlic

8 fresh basil leaves

8 sprigs fresh parsley

Juice of ½ lemon

½ teaspoon Dijon-style
 mustard

Salt and pepper to taste

1 cup olive oil

Salad:

1 pound of your favorite
 shape macaroni

2 tablespoons red wine
 vinegar

1 zucchini, grated

2 celery stalks, finely
 chopped

1 sweet onion, such as
 Vidalia, chopped

½ cup chopped roasted red
 pepper

½ cup chopped chipotle
 peppers

Try making macaroni salad with this Caesar dressing, and use plenty of veggies in it. The kids will love it. Don't be put off by the anchovy paste—it adds a special, indefinable element to the dressing, overlooked by anyone scarred from fishy pizza!

Serves 6 to 8

Put all the dressing ingredients but the oil in the jar of your blender. Whirl on low until pureed. Add the olive oil a little at a time with the motor on low. Refrigerate before using.

Cook the pasta according to package directions. Toss in a bowl with the vinegar.

Add the dressing to the hot pasta. Mix in the rest of the ingredients. Chill, cover, and serve.

Pumpkin Bread

3 eggs

13-ounce can plain pumpkin
   puree

½ cup milk

½ stick butter, melted

2 cups all-purpose flour

2 tablespoons baking
   powder

2 teaspoons dark brown
   sugar

1 teaspoon dried thyme
   leaves

1 teaspoon dried savory

1 teaspoon dried sage leaves

1 teaspoon salt

2 jalapeño peppers, cored,
   seeded, and minced

Black pepper to taste

This can be made sweet or savory. We like the savory version, with some heat and lots of herbs. The sweet version has pumpkin pie spices in it.

Serves 6 to 10

Set your oven at 350 degrees.

Prepare a bread pan with nonstick spray.

Beat the eggs with your electric mixer on low speed, until light and lemon colored. With the motor still running on low, slowly add the liquid ingredients.

Slowly add the dry ingredients, making sure that all is well incorporated. Pour the mixture into the prepared pan.

Bake for 1 hour, or until a toothpick inserted comes out clean.

Arugula Salad with Pecans, Apples, and Swiss Cheese

Vinaigrette:

1 large fresh pear, peeled,
    cored, and chopped

Juice of ½ lemon

2 tablespoons cider vinegar

¾ cup extra-virgin olive oil

Salt and pepper to taste

Salad:

1 cup pecan halves

2 bunches arugula, washed
    and spun dry

2 heads Boston lettuce,
    leaves separated and
    shredded, washed and
    spun dry

2 hard, crisp McIntosh
    apples, cored and
    chopped

4 ounces Swiss cheese,
    cubed or shredded

The secret of this salad is the pear vinaigrette. All of the ingredients yell, "Fall harvest."

Serves 8

Puree the pear and lemon juice in the jar of your blender. Add the cider vinegar and the oil, drop by drop, and process until combined. Taste for salt and pepper. Set aside.

Toast the pecans under your broiler until crisp. Set aside.

Arrange the arugula and lettuce on individual serving plates. Mound the chopped apple on top. Arrange the cheese over the apple. Sprinkle with the reserved pecans. Drizzle with the dressing.

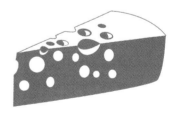

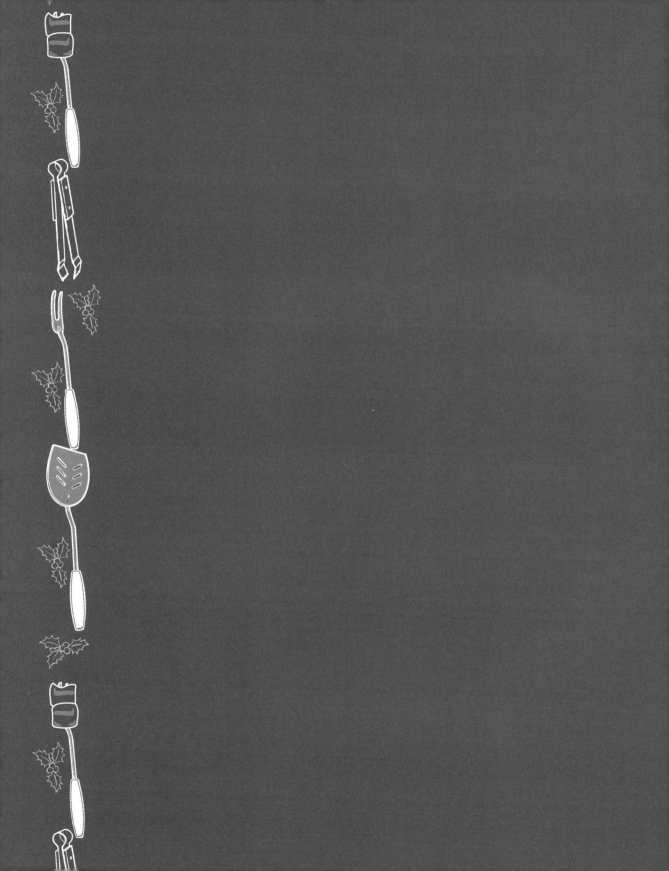

Chapter 11

Make It a Holiday for Two—Romantic BBQ

Okay, caveman, it is you and your woman outside in the wild. You prepare the wood, strike the flint, and build a fire.

Hey, good news! This is the new millennium and you don't have to spark rocks or rub sticks. While you might find that the candlelight dinner indoors for two has its appeal, you can try something very different and romantic with an outdoor meal for just the two of you. Forget the noise and jostling, but cozy up to your loved one with a glass of Pinot Noir and watch the sun as it sets. The two of you can actually put these dishes together with the greatest of ease, and share the experience as well. Not only will you be creating a great meal, but you will be spending precious moments together for the night ahead. Make sure to prepare the decor to your liking, and don't forget the mood lighting!

Grilled Squab

1 cup olive oil

2 cloves garlic, minced

Juice of 1 lemon

½ cup chopped parsley

½ teaspoon dried oregano
leaves

4 squabs, split

Salt and pepper to taste

We find that frozen, split squabs are great for grilling. We cook them with garlic, oil, and herbs for a tasty treat. Serve with Grilled Polenta Patties (see page 197) and a healthy vegetable, such as broccoli. And, there's nothing wrong with picking them up and eating them out of hand!

Serves 2

Heat the olive oil and sauté the garlic for 3 minutes, or until soft. Add the lemon juice and herbs. Remove from the heat.

Sprinkle birds with salt and pepper. Marinate the squabs in the olive oil mixture for 2 hours.

Set your grill at 400 degrees, or use white-hot coals. Grill the squabs for 6 to 8 minutes per side.

Grilled Quail

1 stick unsalted butter
4 tablespoons currant jelly
6 quails
Salt and pepper

The quail is a very small bird and should be served as a delicacy with plenty of other courses. The bird needs to be well browned in order to be perfectly delicious.

Serves 2

Set your grill on high or oven at 450 degrees. Melt the butter and whisk in the jelly.

Rinse the quails under cold water. Pat dry with paper towels. Sprinkle with salt and pepper, inside and out. Dip the birds into the butter mixture to coat.

Roast about 24 minutes, until well browned, basting often.

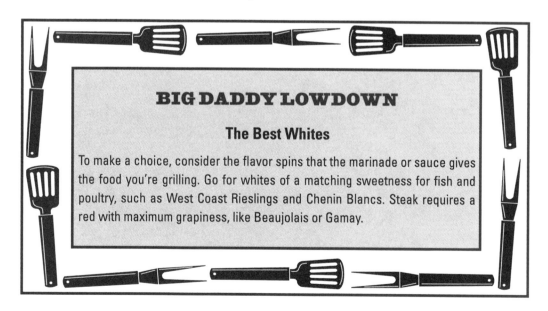

BIG DADDY LOWDOWN

The Best Whites

To make a choice, consider the flavor spins that the marinade or sauce gives the food you're grilling. Go for whites of a matching sweetness for fish and poultry, such as West Coast Rieslings and Chenin Blancs. Steak requires a red with maximum grapiness, like Beaujolais or Gamay.

Skewered Chicken Livers Wrapped in Bacon

8 wooden toothpicks,
  soaked in water
  for 30 minutes
4 slices bacon, blanched
  in boiling water for 2
  minutes, drained on
  paper towels
8 chicken livers, any
  membrane removed
Salt and pepper to taste

Some people like these as hors d'oeuvres; we like to make a meal of chicken livers and bacon.

Makes 8 appetizers

Set your grill at about 350 degrees, or until coals are white-hot.

Cut the bacon slices in halves. Lay the bacon strips out on the towels. Sprinkle the livers with salt and pepper.

Wrap the livers with the bacon and secure with soaked toothpicks.

Grill until the bacon is crisp and the livers are done but still pink inside.

This can be served over rice or on slices of good French or Italian bread.

Grilled Single Pizzas
with Artichokes, Olives, and Muenster

1 pound pizza dough

Topping:

1 box frozen artichoke hearts

1 cup black or kalamata
   olives, pitted and
   chopped

8 ounces Muenster cheese,
   sliced thinly

Hot red pepper flakes

¼ cup olive oil

These are fun for a night of television. Start with two, and bring out two more later in the evening. You can buy the dough in the supermarket or from your local pizza place.

Makes 4 individual pizzas

Set your oven or grill on high (you will bake the pizzas on indirect heat).

Cook the artichokes until soft. Cool, and then chop them, mixing with the chopped olives.

Roll out half the dough into two small rounds, about 5 to 6 inches in diameter, reserving the rest for later.

Lay pieces of the cheese on the dough. Sprinkle with the artichokes, olives, and red pepper flakes.

Drizzle with the olive oil.

Bake until the crust is nicely brown and the cheese has melted into the crust and toppings.

Make the second order of pizzas later!

Grilled Tiny Filets Mignons with Burgundy Sauce

Sauce:

2 tablespoons butter

2 shallots, minced

1 clove garlic, minced

1 cup Burgundy wine

Filets:

4 small medallions of filet
mignon, about 3 to 4
ounces each

Salt and pepper to taste

1 teaspoon bottled steak
sauce, or to taste

The end of the filet is quite skinny. Rolled into medallions and expertly tied, they are tender and delicious. They should be a bit less expensive than the big central cuts of filet.

Serves 2

Set your grill on high, about 400 degrees.

Melt the butter and sauté the shallots and garlic for 5 minutes over low flame.

While the vegetables are cooking, reduce the Burgundy to half. Mix them together.

Let the filets stand out until they reach room temperature, sprinkle with salt and pepper.

Grill the filets about 3 to 4 minutes per side.

Let the filets rest for 6 minutes.

Drizzle with the prepared sauce and serve with mashed potatoes. Use bottled sauce to taste.

BIG DADDY LOWDOWN

Wine with Dinner?

Balance the tastes of fish, chicken, and pork with fruity whites from Germany and Alsace. Gewürztraminer is a great selection. For beef, try mellow low-tannin reds, such as California Merlot and French Côtes du Rhône.

Grilled Salmon Fillet Stuffed, Rolled, and Skewered

2 ounces mascarpone
  cheese, at room
  temperature
1 teaspoon chopped fresh
  chives
2 tablespoons chopped fresh
  dill weed
1 flat salmon fillet, about 12
  to 16 ounces
Juice of ½ lemon
Salt to taste
Plenty of freshly ground
  black pepper
1 tablespoon olive oil

Make sure the salmon fillet is very flat and thin. Each fillet should be about a 5x7-inch oblong. You don't want a big, thick center cut.

Serves 2

Set your grill at 325 degrees.

Mix the mascarpone cheese and the herbs together. Sprinkle the fish with lemon juice, salt, and pepper.

Spread the cheese mixture thinly across the wide side of the fillet and roll it up. Secure with toothpicks. Drizzle with olive oil. Wrap in aluminum foil.

Bake the salmon roll for 20 minutes, until cooked through and the cheese is melted. Cut the roll crosswise in nice pinwheels.

Grilled Fillet of Veal with Mustard Rub

1 veal fillet, about 12 ounces

2 tablespoons butter, melted

Rub:

1 tablespoon dry mustard

1 teaspoon coarse or kosher
  salt

1 tablespoon paprika

1 tablespoon garlic salt

2 tablespoons finely
  chopped fresh rosemary

Freshly ground black pepper
  to taste

You need to know a chef or to go to a specialty butcher to get a fillet of veal. However, it's a most romantic piece of meat, so tender it will melt in your mouth. It's for impressing!

Serves 2

Set your grill on high, about 400 degrees.

Mix the ingredients of the rub together.

Press the rub into the meat and let stand for 1 hour.

Place the meat on the hot grill. Spoon the melted butter over meat. Roast for 4 to 5 minutes per side. Serve medium-rare with Grilled Polenta Patties (see page 197).

Mixed Seafood and Vegetable Kabobs with Ginger-Citrus Sauce

8 wooden skewers, soaked in water for 1 hour

Sauce:

1 teaspoon minced fresh gingerroot

1 tablespoon minced garlic

4 tablespoons orange-juice concentrate, undiluted

4 tablespoons chopped fresh thyme leaves, or 1 tablespoon dried thyme leaves

Juice of ½ lemon

5 tablespoons olive oil

Salt and cayenne pepper to taste

Kabobs:

6 huge diver scallops

6 jumbo shrimp

1 sweet red bell pepper, cut in chunks

4 large white mushrooms, cleaned

The sauce is just different enough to intrigue without blowing away the taste buds!

Serves 2

Place the first 5 sauce ingredients in the jar of your blender. With the motor on low, slowly add the olive oil. Taste for salt and cayenne pepper.

Set your grill on medium-high.

String the seafood and vegetables on the soaked wooden skewers. Paint the kabobs with the sauce.

Grill the kabobs until the shrimp turns pink. Serve with a nice crisp salad.

BIG DADDY LOWDOWN

For Grilling Shish Kebabs

Oil the grill first and rotate shish kebabs while grilling in order to get all sides to cook evenly.

Grilled Chicken Tenders on Skewers with Mushrooms

1 pound chicken tenders,
  rinsed and patted dry on
  paper towels
10 small portobello
  mushrooms
10 slices sweet red onion
Ginger-Citrus Sauce (see
  page 215)

Chicken tenders are the equivalent of the fillet of the chicken. Prepare the sauce as for the previous seafood recipe.

Serves 6 to 8

Set your grill on high.

String the tenders, mushrooms, and onions on metal or soaked wooden skewers. Paint with the sauce.

Grill the skewers for 4 minutes per side.

BIG DADDY LOWDOWN

Dry Rubs

For dry rubs, allow 1 to 2 teaspoons for each serving.

Asparagus and Garnish of Country Ham over Mixed Greens

Bed of mixed baby field
greens, washed and
spun dry

12 ounces asparagus, tips
only (save the stems for
soup)

½ cup of your favorite
vinaigrette

4 ounces country ham, sliced
thin and then minced

This is perfect for two, or make a lot for a crowd. In either event, it's an exciting side to a fabulous meal.

Serves 2

Set your grill on medium-low, about 300 degrees.

Arrange the greens on two attractive salad plates.

String the asparagus crosswise onto 4 metal or soaked wooden skewers.

Brush the asparagus with the dressing and grill for about 20 minutes, or until crisp-tender.

Place the hot asparagus over the greens. Sprinkle with minced ham and use the rest of the dressing to moisten the salad.

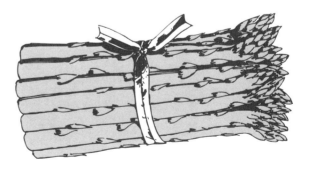

Stuffed Mushrooms

12-ounce box medium-sized
(about 1½ inches across)
button mushrooms, stems
removed

Stuffing:

¼ cup finely chopped onion

2 cloves garlic, finely
chopped

¼ cup olive oil

8 ounces Italian sweet
sausage, steamed and
finely chopped

½ bunch parsley, stems
removed, leaves chopped

2 or 3 slices of good bread,
crusts removed, crumbed
in a food processor to
make 1 cup

Mushrooms can be stuffed with just about anything, from oysters to turkey dressing. We like this one, made with Italian pork sausage, flavored with fennel seeds and fennel. Make lots and freeze them for later.

Serves 4

Set your oven at 350 degrees.

Sauté the onion and garlic in the olive oil. Stir in the sausage and blend well. Add the parsley and bread. Mix well.

Stuff the mushrooms, placing them on a baking sheet. Drizzle with extra oil.

Bake about 12 to 15 minutes, until very hot and steaming.

Baked Risotto with Herbs, Vegetables, and Cheese

1 small sweet onion, about the size of a lemon

1 tablespoon butter

1 tablespoon extra-virgin olive oil

2 teaspoons dried rosemary leaves, or 2 tablespoons chopped fresh rosemary

½ bunch Italian flat-leaf parsley, rinsed, spun dry, and chopped

2 cups short-grain rice

4 cups chicken broth (your own or low-salt canned)

¼ cup white vermouth

1 teaspoon salt

Lots of freshly ground black pepper or to taste

This recipe has been passed down for generations. A CorningWare casserole with a cover works perfectly.

Serves 6

Set your oven at 300 degrees. Sauté the chopped onion in a mixture of butter and olive oil over medium-low heat. Mix in the herbs.

Toss in the rice, coating it with the butter and oil. Slowly add the broth, stirring constantly.

Add the vermouth, salt, and pepper.

Bake, covered, for 60 minutes, stirring every 20 minutes.

Do not burn. If the rice gets too dry, add more broth or water.

Creamed Baby Onions and Pattypan Squash

1 pound tiny white onions, ¾ to 1 inch in diameter, root ends cut off

1 pound pattypan squash, washed, left whole

13-ounce can low-salt chicken broth

1 cup heavy or whipping cream

1 tablespoon Wondra quick-blending flour

¼ teaspoon ground nutmeg

Salt and pepper to taste

¼ cup bread crumbs

Pattypan squash is a tiny version of winter squash. Most growers thought the miniature squash just did not want to grow, so it was thrown out for generations. Today, the squash is prized as a delicacy. Pattypan squash abounds in many gardens, growing unbidden into tiny, pale yellow or soft green jewels. Like a watercolor painting, it is special.

Serves 4

Place the onions and squash in a saucepan with the chicken broth. Cover and simmer gently until fork-tender.

Remove the onions and squash. Reduce the broth by ¼. Add the cream and reduce by half (about 1¼ cups). Stir in the flour, nutmeg, salt, and pepper.

Pour cream sauce over vegetables. Serve plain, or sprinkle with bread crumbs and run under the broiler.

BIG DADDY LOWDOWN

Baby Onions

Little onions come into season for Thanksgiving—but you can get them year-round or grow them yourself. They are a pain to peel, but it's worth it to use fresh ones, as the frozen baby onions are mushy.

Waffles as Bases for Creamed Seafood

Two 8-inch waffles, well
    toasted
2 teaspoons butter
1 shallot, minced or chopped
2 teaspoons Wondra quick-
    blending flour
¼ cup cream
¼ cup bottled clam juice
½ teaspoon Worcestershire
    sauce
8 ounces cooked shrimp,
    chopped
Salt and pepper to taste
½ teaspoon dry dill weed

If you make waffles for breakfast, you always have a few too many, so freeze the extras! Or use frozen waffles, but make sure that you toast them until they are very crisp. This is a marvelous supper or intimate brunch with champagne!

Serves 2

Toast the waffles and place on warm plates.

Melt the butter and sauté the shallot. Stir in the flour and cook for 4 minutes. Add the cream, whisking until thick. Whisk in the clam juice. When thickened, add the rest of the ingredients. Stir to mix well and spoon over hot waffles. Serve immediately.

Skewered Cherry Tomatoes Grilled with Herb, Anchovy, and Oil Dressing

Dressing:

2 tablespoons lemon juice

3 tablespoons extra-virgin
   olive oil

1 clove garlic, minced

½ inch anchovy paste

4 fresh basil leaves, torn

½ teaspoon dried oregano
   leaves

Salt and pepper to taste

10 cherry tomatoes

Four 8-inch wooden
   skewers, soaked in water
   for 1 hour

You can use regular, largish, red cherry tomatoes, but try to find the yellow ones.

Serves 2

Set your grill on medium.

Whisk the dressing ingredients, or whirl them in the jar of your blender.

Cut the stem ends off the tomatoes and squeeze out some of the juices and seeds. Soak the tomatoes in the dressing.

String the tomatoes on the skewers. Grill until very hot and sizzling.

Baby Eggplants Grilled with Fresh Mint and Lemon

Lemon-infused oil:

1 cup olive oil

Peel of 1 lemon

Juice of 1 lemon

Eggplant:

2 to 3 baby eggplants, cut in
  half lengthwise

6 teaspoons lemon-infused
  oil (see above)

6 fresh mint leaves, chopped

Salt and pepper to taste

When you make lemon-infused oil, you'll find a burst of flavor you can use in lots of different dishes, from salad dressings to seafood to chicken. This recipe makes 1 cup of oil, but you will use only a couple of spoonfuls with the eggplant.

Serves 2

Heat the oil, but do not boil. Add the lemon peel and juice. Let cool.

Strain and bottle the oil for future use.

Set your grill on medium-high. While it's heating, take a fork and score the eggplants.

Drizzle the eggplants with the lemon-infused oil, mint, salt, and pepper, pushing into the flesh with the back of a fork or spoon.

When the oil has absorbed, grill the eggplants cut side down for about 4 minutes, or until they start to have nice brown grill marks. Turn and grill for about 2 minutes on the skin side.

Baby Okra Mini-Gumbo

1 tablespoon butter

1 tablespoon all-purpose
flour

2 tablespoons minced onion

2 tablespoons minced green
bell pepper

2 tablespoons finely
chopped celery

½ cup chopped fresh tomato

½ teaspoon filé powder

4 baby okra, coarsely
chopped

1 teaspoon green
peppercorns

Salt and pepper to taste

This is great when you need a good fresh-tasting vegetable to go with fish or seafood.

Serves 2

In a skillet over low heat, make a roux with the butter and flour, stirring until lightly browned. Add the onion, pepper, and celery. Let the vegetables soften over low heat.

Stir in the rest of the ingredients. Cover and simmer for 15 to 20 minutes.

Stuffed Croissants

1 tablespoon butter or oil

2 shallots, minced

4 large mushrooms, stemmed, cleaned, and chopped

2 ounces prosciutto ham

¼ cup chopped parsley

¼ cup heavy or whipping cream

Pinch ground nutmeg

Pepper to taste

2 jumbo croissants, or 4 medium ones, split lengthwise

You'll need the big, puffy commercial croissants to make this dish. Fortunately, jumbo croissants are available at many bakeries and supermarkets.

Serves 2

Melt the butter or heat the oil in a saucepan. Stir in the shallots and sauté about 5 minutes, until they are softened. Add the rest of the ingredients, stirring.

Toast the croissants. Fill with the mushroom mixture. Serve for midnight supper with champagne.

You can make the filling in advance, just reheat it when you are ready to eat.

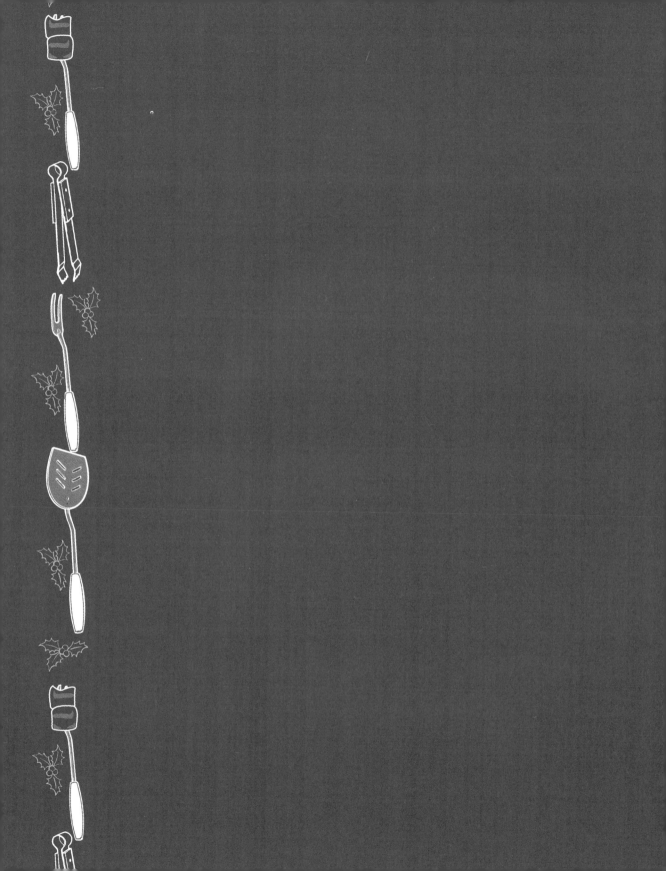

Chapter 12

Desserts

Let's face it. A meal's just not a meal without dessert. We're not going to put our heads in the sand and tell you to run out for Häagen Dazs. Oh, yeah, make sure there's ice cream in the freezer, but for the imaginative grill chef, the sky is the limit.

We like to do fun things with fruits on the grill, smothered with honey or sweet with sugar. And you can bet your bottom dollar that the holiday audience you're catering to is going to want something with chocolate! Here's a divine, delectable selection—some prepared on the grill, some not.

Pumpkin Pie

1-crust pie shell, your own,
    commercial frozen, or
    refrigerated

4 extra-large eggs

13-ounce can pumpkin, or
    two 10-ounce boxes
    frozen winter squash,
    cooked down to 2 cups
    and cooled

1 cup heavy or whipping
    cream

¼ cup packed dark brown
    sugar, or to taste (some
    like it sweet!)

1 teaspoon ground cinnamon

½ teaspoon ground nutmeg

1 teaspoon minced fresh
    gingerroot

¼ teaspoon ground cloves

¼ teaspoon ground allspice

1 teaspoon salt

Our family loves pumpkin pie so much that we have it all fall and winter long. This is a very spicy recipe, so a scoop of vanilla ice cream or some whipped cream with a tad of vanilla and sugar in it make a terrific counterpoint.

Serves 8

Prepare a 9-inch glass pie plate with nonstick spray. Line the prepared pie plate with pie shell. Set your oven at 400 degrees.

Using your electric mixer, beat the eggs in a large bowl. Add the pumpkin. With the motor running, whirl in the rest of the ingredients.

Pour the filling into the pie shell and bake at 400 degrees for 15 minutes. Turn the heat down to 325 degrees and bake for 55 minutes.

President's Day Cherry Clafouti

Cherries:

3 cups fresh cherries, pitted

½ cup rosé wine

2 tablespoons white sugar

Flan:

¾ cup milk

4 large or extra-large eggs

¼ cup white sugar (¼ cup more if you are using sour red cherries)

1 teaspoon vanilla extract

½ teaspoon kosher salt

1 cup all-purpose flour

Cherries soaked in rosé wine then baked into a country flan makes a terrific dessert! It helps to have a cherry pitter and fabulous cherry crop! Once we mixed red pie cherries with black cherries. What a great combo. If you are using some pie cherries, add ¼ cup extra sugar—they are sour!

Serves 8 to 10

Soak the cherries in the wine and sugar for 1 hour.

Set your oven at 350 degrees. Prepare a glass pie plate with nonstick spray. Set aside.

Whirl the flan ingredients in the jar of your blender, stopping every 20 seconds to scrape down the sides.

Pour ¼ inch of the flan mixture in the prepared pie plate. Place in the oven for 5 minutes, or until it sets.

Sprinkle the cherry mixture in the pan with the skim of flan. Pour in the rest of the flan batter.

Bake for about 1 hour. The clafouti will puff and be lovely to dump ice cream or whipped cream on top.

Strawberry Shortcake

12 of your favorite biscuits, 2 for each big adult, 1 for each child

Berries:

4 cups fresh strawberries

½ cup white sugar

Whipped cream:

1 cup heavy or whipping cream

½ cup white sugar

1 teaspoon vanilla extract

Most people today think that cream comes from a can. Here's a recipe for delicious whipped cream, and once you've made it yourself, you'll skip the canned stuff. Be sure to give the kids the beaters to lick!

Serves 6

Wash the strawberries. Reserve 12 perfect ones for decoration. Hull and slice the remaining berries. Place in a bowl with the sugar, the whole ones on top for easy access. Cover and refrigerate for 30 minutes.

Using your electric mixer on low, whip the cream until it starts to form soft peaks.

Slowly add the sugar and then the vanilla. Important: Do not overbeat! If you overbeat the cream, you will make sweetened butter!

To assemble, split the hot biscuits, reserving one half of each as a "hat." Place 1 or 2 halves on each plate.

Spoon the whipped cream over the hot biscuits. Add the sliced strawberries. Top with the second half of the biscuit, spoon on more of the whipped cream, and decorate with the whole berries for a great look.

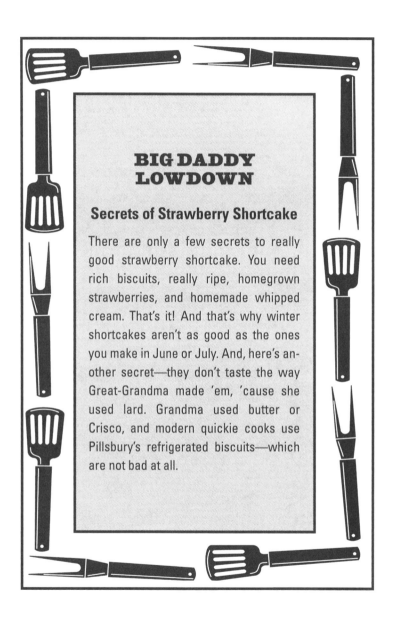

BIG DADDY LOWDOWN

Secrets of Strawberry Shortcake

There are only a few secrets to really good strawberry shortcake. You need rich biscuits, really ripe, homegrown strawberries, and homemade whipped cream. That's it! And that's why winter shortcakes aren't as good as the ones you make in June or July. And, here's another secret—they don't taste the way Great-Grandma made 'em, 'cause she used lard. Grandma used butter or Crisco, and modern quickie cooks use Pillsbury's refrigerated biscuits—which are not bad at all.

Red, White, and Blue Pudding (White Chocolate with Raspberries and Blueberries)

6 ounces white chocolate

1 envelope unflavored gelatin

¼ cup cool water

⅔ cup powdered sugar, or to taste

⅔ cup cold milk

1 teaspoon salt

4 egg whites

1 cup heavy or whipping cream

1 teaspoon vanilla extract

½ pint raspberries, rinsed and dried on paper towels

1 pint blueberries, rinsed and dried on paper towels

Mint sprigs, for garnish

This is as much a mousse as a pudding; however, a mousse or pudding under any other name would taste as sweet!

Serves 8 to 10

Melt the chocolate in a pan over a base pan of simmering water. When the chocolate is almost melted, stir until completely smooth. Remove from the heat.

Place the gelatin and water in the jar of your blender. Let the gelatin soften.

With the motor on low, add the melted white chocolate. Slowly add the powdered sugar, milk, and salt.

Pour the mixture into a large bowl. Let cool while you beat the egg whites until stiff.

Fold the egg whites into the white chocolate mixture.

In a separate bowl, beat the cream and add the vanilla when peaks are just beginning to form. Fold the cream into the white chocolate mixture. Refrigerate for at least 3 hours, stirring every 30 minutes. Fold in the berries.

Serve in cocktail glasses. Decorate with sprigs of mint.

Make Your Own Sundae Dessert Buffet

Per person:

6 ounces (2 scoops) ice
cream (strawberry,
vanilla, chocolate, butter
pecan, coffee, etc.—
make them age-
appropriate)

Toppings

Whipped cream (see page
230)

This is about the best thing you can do for a children's party! You can use warmers heated by candles for hot fudge and hot butterscotch. All kinds of fruits for toppings are served in bowls and grown-ups scoop out the ice cream, sauces, and such yummy treats as chocolate sprinkles, chocolate chips, nuts, and tiny marshmallows. Candy silver balls are attractive, too, as is a big pot of freshly whipped cream. Serve in old-fashioned sundae glasses, which are very attractive and good for older folks' memories of ice-cream parlors.

Grilled Nectarines with Mascarpone

4 large firm, ripe nectarines

4 teaspoons white sugar

1 cup mascarpone cheese

1 tablespoon white sugar

2 tablespoons orange-
flavored liqueur

Nectarines, sweet and fresh, are wonderful grilled. They can be a savory accompaniment to meat, poultry, or seafood—or they can be used as a sweet dessert.

Serves 4

Set your grill on high. Wash the nectarines, cut them in half, and twist to remove the pit, but leave the skins on.

Sprinkle each nectarine half with the 4 teaspoons white sugar. Place cut side down on the grill and cook about 3 minutes, until they form marks.

Mix the mascarpone cheese with the 1 tablespoon white sugar and the orange liqueur.

When the fruit is cooked, spoon the cheese mixture into pit holes. Serve with extra dashes of orange liqueur.

Grilled Grapefruit with Honey and Nuts

3 large grapefruit, halved, seeds removed, and sectioned for easy eating

6 teaspoons good-quality honey

¾ cup chopped nuts

3 teaspoons butter

This is a fine brunch dish. You can cut the sections in advance with a grapefruit spoon or sharp knife and just run under the broiler at the last minute.

Serves 6

Set your grill or broiler on high. Cover the bottom of a baking pan with aluminum foil. Place the prepared grapefruit on the baking pan.

Drizzle honey on the grapefruit, sprinkle with nuts, and dot with butter.

Cook until the nuts have browned and the grapefruit is sizzling hot. Serve hot.

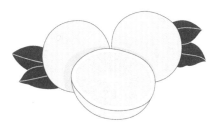

Grilled Orange Slices with Fudge Sauce

8 large oranges

4 teaspoons white sugar

4 tablespoons lemon juice

4 cups orange sherbet or
   sorbet

2 cups hot fudge sauce
   (commercial from a jar is
   fine)

This is a hot-cold-hot dessert, and wonderful!

Serves 8

Prepare a pie plate with nonstick spray.

Peel and section the oranges. Place in the prepared pie plate. Sprinkle with the sugar and lemon juice. Run under your broiler until the sugar caramelizes. Spoon into cocktail glasses.

Scoop some orange sherbet or sorbet over the hot oranges.

Heat the fudge sauce and drizzle over the oranges.

Plum Mousse

2 envelopes unflavored
  gelatin
½ cup cool water
6 red or purple plums
½ to 1 cup white sugar
1½ cups water
1 cup heavy or whipping
  cream, whipped with 2
  tablespoons powdered
  sugar

This is so very attractive, and really good to make when you have lots of plums on the trees. Serve in wineglasses, stacking the ingredients.

Serves 6

Place the gelatin in the jar of your blender. Add the cool water and let the gelatin soften.

Put the plums, sugar, and water in a saucepan, bring to a boil, and lower the heat. Simmer for 6 to 8 minutes, or until the plums are soft. Pour the liquid into the jar of your blender and whirl until pureed.

When the plums are cool enough to handle, remove and discard the pits, leaving the skin on.

Put the fruit in your blender and spin until pureed. Let cool.

Whip the cream. Put alternate spoonfuls of plum puree and whipped cream in wineglasses. Serve chilled.

Blackberry Sauce for Ice Cream

1 quart blackberries,
   stemmed and rinsed in
   cold water
2 cups cold water
1 cup white sugar, or to taste
¼ lemon, juice and skin

Because blackberries have so many seeds, many people miss the delights of fresh, juicy berries in deep summer.

Place all the ingredients in a saucepan, bring to a boil, then lower the heat.

Simmer, covered, for 15 minutes.

Let cool, then push through a strainer. Keep as much of the lemon pulp as possible, discarding all of the seeds.

Cool and store in a closed jar.

Hot Chocolate–Cherry Brownie Sundaes

Brownies:

1 stick butter

4 ounces bittersweet
  chocolate

2 large eggs

1½ cups white sugar

1 teaspoon pure vanilla
  extract

2 tablespoons cherry
  liqueur

¾ cup all-purpose flour

½ teaspoon baking
  powder

½ teaspoon salt

½ can sour pie cherries,
  drained

**To assemble the
sundaes:**

10 sundae glasses, chilled

10 small scoops vanilla
  ice cream

10 small scoops chocolate
  ice cream

Brownie crumbs, warmed

2 cups heavy or whipping
  cream, whipped (see
  page 230)

These brownies are for grown-ups and not really what kids enjoy. If you decide to make the brownies in advance, just pop them in the microwave for a few seconds to heat them up at serving time. Also, you can buy old-fashioned ice-cream parlor sundae glasses on the Web.

Serves 10

Set your oven at 350 degrees. Prepare a 9-inch square baking pan with nonstick spray.

Melt the butter and chocolate together in a saucepan over very low heat.

Cool the butter mixture until lukewarm.

Using your electric mixer, beat together the eggs, sugar, vanilla, and cherry liqueur. When smooth, slowly add the flour, baking powder, and salt. Add chocolate and butter mixture.

Spread the mixture in the prepared baking pan and dot the mixture with cherries, pushing them into the batter.

Bake for 35 to 40 minutes. Cool completely on a wire rack. Crumble the brownies for use in the sundaes.

Place a tablespoon of the crumbs in the bottom of each glass. Add a scoop of vanilla ice cream and a teaspoon of the crumbs, then a scoop of chocolate ice cream to each glass. Sprinkle with remaining crumbs and spoon on the whipped cream.

Orange and Lemon Cheesecake
with Chocolate-Hazelnut Crust

Crust:

¾ cup hazelnuts, toasted

¾ cup dark chocolate wafers

4 teaspoons powdered sugar

1 stick unsalted butter,
   melted

Filling:

Three 8-ounce packages
   cream cheese (not low-
   fat), at room temperature

1 cup white sugar

4 extra-large eggs

½ teaspoon salt

¼ cup freshly squeezed
   lemon juice

2 tablespoons orange liqueur
   or orange-juice
   concentrate

1 tablespoon finely grated
   lemon peel

1 tablespoon finely grated
   orange peel

Whole fresh mint leaves, for
   garnish

This is a real festive dessert that is wonderfully refreshing for a summer holiday party.

Serves 10 to 12

Set your oven at 325 degrees. Prepare a 9-inch springform pan with nonstick spray. Set aside.

Place the toasted nuts and the chocolate wafers in the bowl of your food processor. Whirl until ground, adding the powdered sugar a teaspoonful at a time and the melted butter in a thin stream. Pulse until well blended.

Press the crust mixture into the bottom and ½ inch up the side of the prepared pan. Refrigerate until ready to bake.

Using your electric mixer, beat the cream cheese until smooth. Slowly add the white sugar.

Beat in the eggs one at a time. Mix in the rest of the ingredients, one at a time.

Pour into the prepared springform pan. Bake for 1 hour. Turn off oven. Crack oven door and finish baking for another hour. Let cool and then refrigerate overnight. Garnish slices with fresh mint leaves.